# SMOOTHIES RECIPES

Quick and Delicious Recipes Cookbook for Optimize Your Health

(Healthy Delicious Smoothies Recipes for Weight Loss Managing Diabetes)

**Marta Pantoja**

Published by Sharon Lohan

# © Marta Pantoja

All Rights Reserved

*Smoothies Recipes: Quick and Delicious Recipes Cookbook for Optimize Your Health (Healthy Delicious Smoothies Recipes for Weight Loss Managing Diabetes)*

**ISBN 978-1-990334-43-6**

All rights reserved. No part of this guide may be reproduced in any form without permission in writing from the publisher except in the case of brief quotations embodied in critical articles or reviews.

**Legal & Disclaimer**

The information contained in this book is not designed to replace or take the place of any form of medicine or professional medical advice. The information in this book has been provided for educational and entertainment purposes only.

The information contained in this book has been compiled from sources deemed reliable, and it is accurate to the best of the Author's knowledge; however, the Author cannot guarantee its accuracy and validity and cannot be held liable for any errors or omissions. Changes are periodically made to this book. You must consult your doctor or get professional medical advice before using any of the suggested remedies, techniques, or information in this book.

# Table of contents

Part 1 .................................................................................................... 1
Introduction ......................................................................................... 2
Celery Smoothie With Banana And Carrots ..................................... 3
Celery With Smoothies And Carrots And Apple .............................. 4
Celery Smoothies With Tomatoes And Apples ................................ 5
Smoothies Of Celery With Kiwi And Apple ...................................... 6
Smoothies Of Celery With Cucumber ............................................... 7
Spinach Drink With Kiwi Fruit ........................................................... 8
"Velvet Freshness" .............................................................................. 9
Broccoli And Avocado ...................................................................... 10
Lime Green Smoothies ..................................................................... 11
Healthy Cocktail Health ................................................................... 12
Smoothies For Weight Loss ............................................................. 13
Detox Smoothies With Strawberries And Beets ........................... 14
Slick Smoothie With Kiwi And Celery ............................................. 15
Smoothies With Raspberries And Orange ..................................... 16
Yogurt With Rhubarb ....................................................................... 17
Smoothies With Strawberries And Rhubarb ................................. 18
Pumpkin With Cinnamon ................................................................ 19
Pumpkin With Oat Flakes ................................................................ 20
Pumpkin With Spices ....................................................................... 21
Carrot With Spinach ......................................................................... 22
Carrots With Parsley ........................................................................ 23
Carrots With Celery .......................................................................... 24

Creamy Smoothies With Nuts And Dried Fruits .......................... 25

Cocktail "Good Health" ................................................................. 26

Detox Smoothies With Strawberries And Beets ......................... 27

Slick Smoothie With Kiwi And Celery ......................................... 28

Smoothies With Raspberries And Orange ................................. 29

Yogurt With Rhubarb .................................................................... 30

Smoothies With Strawberries And Rhubarb .............................. 31

Pumpkin With Cinnamon ............................................................. 32

Pumpkin With Oat Flakes ............................................................. 33

Pumpkin With Spices .................................................................... 34

Carrot With Spinach ..................................................................... 35

Carrots With Parsley .................................................................... 36

Carrots With Celery ..................................................................... 37

Creamy Smoothies With Nuts And Dried Fruits .......................... 38

Cocktail "Good Health" ................................................................. 39

Oatmeal Smoothies ...................................................................... 40

November Smoothies With Persimmons .................................... 41

Mandarin Smoothies .................................................................... 42

Grape And Cherry Smoothies ...................................................... 43

Mango-Pineapple Smoothies ...................................................... 44

Blueberry-Buckwheat Smoothies ............................................... 45

Sea-Buckthorn-Calyon Smoothies ............................................. 46

Pomegranate Smoothies With Orange ....................................... 47

Cranberry Smoothies ................................................................... 48

Beetroot Latte ............................................................................... 49

Cedar Smoothies With Cherries And Chocolate ........................ 50

Sesame-orange milkshake .......................................................... 51

Sesame Smoothies With Berries .................................................................. 52
Smoothie Recipe ............................................................................................ 53
1: The Green Mango Booster .................................................................... 53
2: Berry Orange Creamsicle Smoothie ..................................................... 54
3. Strawberry Banana Protein Blast ........................................................ 55
4. Fruity Spinach Green Smoothie ........................................................... 56
5. Post Workout Melon Berry Smoothie ................................................. 57
6. Blueberry Power Smoothie ................................................................... 58
7. Kale, Berry And Acai Power Smoothie ............................................... 59
8. Cherry Bakewell Protein Smoothie ..................................................... 60
9. Green Warrior Protein Smoothie ......................................................... 61
10. Raw Caramel Apple Smoothie (Vegan, Gluten Free) .................... 62
11. Grapefruit Ginger Citrus Green Smoothie ...................................... 63
12. Creamy Turmeric Smoothie ................................................................ 64
13. Banana Coconut Cream ....................................................................... 65
14. Walnut Pineapple Workout Replenisher ......................................... 66
15. Blueberry Avocado And Spinach Smoothie .................................... 67
Smoothies For Weight Loss ....................................................................... 68
2. Chocolate Peanut Butter Banana Breakfast Smoothie .................. 69
3. Green Breakfast Blast ............................................................................. 70
4. Spinach And Avocado Smoothie ......................................................... 71
5. Chocolate Chia Cherry Smoothie ........................................................ 72
6. Banana And Coconut Water ................................................................. 73
7. Carrot Cake Smoothie (Gluten-Free + Vegan) ................................. 74
8. Red Velvet Beet Smoothie .................................................................... 75
9. Kiwi Green Smoothie ............................................................................. 76
10. Anti-Inflammatory Green Smoothie With Turmeric .................... 77

11. Strawberry, Banana And Green Tea Smoothie ........... 78
12. Peanut Butter Smoothie ........................................... 79
13. Mango Smoothie ...................................................... 80
14. Almond Orange Smoothie ....................................... 81
15. C-Blast Smoothie ..................................................... 82
16. Strawberry Chia Watermelon Smoothie ................. 83
17. Banana Ginger Smoothie ......................................... 84
18. Mocha Smoothie ...................................................... 85
19. Mulberry, Lavender, And Kale Energizing Smoothie ........ 86
20. Orange Papaya Passion Fruit .................................. 87
21. Spicy Grapefruit Pineapple ..................................... 88
Banana Auburn Smoothie ............................................. 89
Orange Dream ................................................................ 90
Green Blueberry Banana Drink ..................................... 91
Berry Breakfast .............................................................. 93
Best of the World .......................................................... 95
Pineapple Desire ............................................................ 96
Kiwi Strawberry Smoothie ............................................ 97
BBS Smoothie ................................................................. 99
Tropical Perfection ...................................................... 101
Simply Peachy .............................................................. 102
Morning Madness ........................................................ 104
Watermelon Miracle ................................................... 106
Berry Nice Workout Drink .......................................... 107
Sunrise Drink ............................................................... 109
Berry Plain Sensation .................................................. 110
Tutti Frutti ................................................................... 112

| | |
|---|---|
| Luscious Smoothie | 113 |
| Slim Down Smoothie | 115 |
| Noble Soy Smoothie | 116 |
| Mango Folly | 118 |
| Super Green | 119 |
| Healthy Kale | 121 |
| Sweet Soul | 122 |
| Smoothie Bliss | 123 |
| Smooth Green Drink | 124 |
| Crazy Sensual Goddess | 125 |
| Strawberry Meadows | 126 |
| Sicilian Carrot | 127 |
| Blue Lemon | 128 |
| Strawberry Goji | 129 |
| Blue Ginger | 130 |
| Mint Berry | 131 |
| Sexy Detox | 132 |
| Super Fresh Green | 133 |
| Glowing Blast | 134 |
| Clear Sip Smoothie | 135 |
| Berry Pick-Me-Up | 136 |
| Forever Young | 137 |
| Cranberry Smoothie | 138 |
| Fat Booty Buster | 139 |
| Berry Pomegranate Smoothie | 140 |
| Gentle Wind | 142 |
| Hawaiian Drink | 143 |

Part 2 .................................................................................................. 146

Introduction .................................................................................. 147

Chapter 1: Smoothies With Benefits ........................................ 149

Chapter 2: How To Make Smoothies? .................................... 152

Chapter 3: Smoothie Ingredients For Weight Loss ................ 155

Chapter 4: Beginners Plan. Smoothie Recipes For Days 1 To 7 .................................................................................................. 160

Day One ........................................................................................ 161

Spiced Apple Smoothie ............................................................. 161

Three Berry Smoothie ................................................................ 162

Day Two ....................................................................................... 163

Spiced Banana Smoothie .......................................................... 163

Very Cherry Smoothie ............................................................... 164

Day Three .................................................................................... 165

Berry Red Smoothie ................................................................... 166

Day Four ...................................................................................... 167

Easy Blueberry Smoothie .......................................................... 167

Choco Peanut Smoothie ........................................................... 168

Day Five ....................................................................................... 169

Avocado Mango Smoothie ....................................................... 169

Nutty Raspberry Smoothie ....................................................... 170

Day Six ......................................................................................... 171

Berry Avocado Smoothie .......................................................... 171

Savory Carrot Smoothie ............................................................ 172

Day Seven .................................................................................... 173

Berry Chia Smoothie .................................................................. 173

Berry Nutty Smoothie ................................................................ 174

Chapter 5: Smoothie Recipes For Days 8 To 14 ......................... 175

Day Eight .................................................................................. 176

Coco Raspberry Smoothie ..................................................... 176

Creamy Blueberry Smoothie ................................................. 177

Day Nine .................................................................................. 178

Coco Choco Smoothie ............................................................ 178

Apple Kale Smoothie .............................................................. 179

Day Ten .................................................................................... 180

All-Green Smoothie ................................................................ 180

Mint Green Smoothie ............................................................. 181

Day Eleven ............................................................................... 182

Spiced Green Apple Smoothie ............................................... 182

Tangy Minty Green Smoothie ................................................ 183

Day Twelve .............................................................................. 184

Coco Kale Smoothie ............................................................... 184

Sweet Green Tea Smoothie ................................................... 185

Day Thirteen ............................................................................ 186

Spinach Berry Smoothie ........................................................ 186

Creamy Blackberry Smoothie ................................................ 187

Day Fourteen ................................... **Error! Bookmark not defined.**

Green Herb Smoothie ................ **Error! Bookmark not defined.**

Tangy Creamy Smoothie ............ **Error! Bookmark not defined.**

Chapter 6: Bonus Smoothie-Making Tips ...... **Error! Bookmark not defined.**

Spinach Orange recipe ............... **Error! Bookmark not defined.**

Orange Kale Protein Green Juice Recipe ........ **Error! Bookmark not defined.**

Conclusion.........................................................................................188

# Part 1

# Introduction

Smoothies are a concentrate of vitamins and fiber in one glass. After all, in one serving of smoothies, several vegetables or fruits can be placed at once. That's why to be bored for breakfast and at any time - to weakened people. Smoothie is like a clever food designer. You can collect a dish that solves those or other problems of a particular person.

# Celery Smoothie With Banana And Carrots

**Ingredients:**

- celery - 100 g;
- banana - one piece;
- carrots - one piece;
- honey - a teaspoon;
- cinnamon - 3 g;
- kefir - 25 ml;
- parsley - 50 g (optional);
- water - 50 ml.

**Preparation:**

1. First of all, wash the celery well and separate the stem. To facilitate the grinding process, remove the coarse fibers, and cut the stem into small pieces. Load the blender into the bowl.
2. Remove from the banana peel, break into pieces and send to celery.
3. Next, you need to prepare the carrots. To do this, wash it well and remove the top layer. Slice it with thin half rings and add to the celery and banana.
4. Porridge thoroughly washed and chopped with a knife, also send into the blender bowl.
5. Then add the rest of the ingredients: honey, kefir, water, cinnamon.
6. Turn on the blender until the ingredients are completely ground into a homogeneous mass.

## Celery With Smoothies And Carrots And Apple
**Ingredients:**

- Necessary ingredients:
- Apple - 200 g;
- Carrots - 100 g;
- Celery - 150 g.

**Preparation:**

1. First of all, wash thoroughly and dry all ingredients.
2. Carrots clean from the top layer and cut into thin semicircles.
3. Stem the celery free from coarse fibers and cut into slices.
4. Mix all the ingredients in the bowl and turn on the blender for a while, until a uniform pulp is formed.
5. The received smoothies not only will please with taste, but also will charge an organism with energy, and also will strengthen immune system.

# Celery Smoothies With Tomatoes And Apples

**Ingredients:**

- Necessary ingredients:
- Apple - 200-250 g;
- Carrots - 100 g;
- Celery - 150 g;
- Tomatoes - 200 g.

**Preparation:**

1. Apple to wash, peel off from it and cut into small pieces, after removing the bones.
2. Carrots must first be boiled and cooled, remove the top layer from it and cut into pieces.
3. Stem the celery from the coarse fibers and cut into pieces.
4. With tomatoes peel off. To facilitate this process, preliminarily pass the fetus with boiling water. Next, wipe it through a sieve, so that the seeds do not hit the smoothies.
5. All the prepared components are loaded into the blender bowl and turned on until a homogeneous mass is formed.

## Smoothies Of Celery With Kiwi And Apple

**Ingredients:**

- Necessary ingredients:
- The stalk of celery;
- Green apple - one piece;
- Kiwi - one piece;
- Water - 100 ml;
- Honey - optional.

**Preparation:**

1. Prepare the stalk of celery: rinse and dry it, and also remove coarse fibers and cut the stem into pieces.
2. With apples peel and remove the seed box, cut into small pieces.
3. Kiwi peel and cut into several pieces.
4. Prepared components are loaded into the blender bowl, add honey and water.
5. Beat all ingredients with a blender until smooth.
6. Adding honey is not necessary, but if you are a sweetie, one spoon will brighten the sour taste of apples and kiwi and make your smoothies sour-sweet.

# Smoothies Of Celery With Cucumber

**Ingredients:**

- Necessary ingredients:
- Stem of celery - 100 g;
- Half a lemon;
- Apple green - one piece;
- One banana;
- Cucumber - 150 g;
- Purified water - 200 ml.

**Preparation:**

1. Prepare the celery: wash and dry with a napkin, remove coarse fibers and cut into pieces.
2. Remove the apple from the apple and remove the bones, also cut into small pieces.
3. Cucumber clean - peel, it is convenient to do with a vegetable peeler. Cut into slices.
4. Banana peel and break into pieces.
5. Mix all the ingredients in the bowl of the blender until a puree consistency is formed.

## Spinach Drink With Kiwi Fruit

**Ingredients:**

- To prepare 2 servings, take:
- 2 small bunches of spinach;
- 1 medium fruit of kiwi fruit;
- ½ ripe banana.

**Preparation:**

1. Mix all the ingredients in a thick cocktail with a dip or a blender cup.

## "Velvet Freshness"

**Ingredients:**

- To create this drink you need:
- 1 medium avocado (pulp);
- 1 small green apple;
- 1 small cucumber.

**Preparation:**

1. Get the flesh of the avocado, cucumber and apple to rid the skin. All the ingredients cut into cubes and put into a combine.
2. Using a blender, prepare a thick, homogeneous mashed potatoes.

# Broccoli And Avocado

**Ingredients:**

- For a magic drink you will need:
-  slightly boiled (can be raw) inflorescences of broccoli - 3-4 pcs .;
- 1 large avocado;
- low-fat creamy yogurt - 1/3 cup.

**Preparation:**

1. Mix all ingredients with a blender. Finished product decorate with a slice of cucumber or lime.

# Lime Green Smoothies

**Ingredients:**

- For the preparation of an invigorating drink you need to take:
- 1 medium lime (pulp and zest);
- 1 large green apple;
- 4-5 ice cubes.

**Preparation:**

1. Mix all ingredients with a blender. Finished product with a sprig of mint and lime.

# Healthy Cocktail Health

**Ingredients:**

- To create an incredibly delicious drink you need:
- 150 grams of fresh pineapple (cubes);
- 1 medium fruit of kiwi fruit;
- 1 medium cucumber.

**Preparation:**

1. Remove all ingredients from the skin and cut into cubes. With a blender, whisk the drink into a thick foam.

# Smoothies For Weight Loss

**Ingredients:**

- 1 medium stalk of celery;
- 1 large apple;
- natural lemon juice - 1/3 cup;
- greens (parsley + dill);
- mint fresh - to taste.

**Preparation:**

1. Mix all ingredients with a blender and dilute with lemon juice.

## Detox Smoothies With Strawberries And Beets
**Ingredients:**

- Water - 1 tbsp. (or coconut water)
- Strawberry - 1 tbsp. (can be frozen)
- Avocado - 1/2 pcs.
- Beets - 1/2 tbsp.
- Apple - 1 pc.
- Lemon juice - 1 tbsp.

**Preparation:**

1. Peel the beet and apple, cut into large pieces. Beat all ingredients until smooth.

# Slick Smoothie With Kiwi And Celery

**Ingredients:**

- Celery - 4 stems
- Kiwi - 6-8 pieces.
- Millet flakes - ½ tbsp.
- Salt, cinnamon, lemon juice - to taste
- Honey or maple syrup
- Watercress

**Preparation:**

1. Kiwis cleaned. Millet flakes boil with boiling water until thick porridge. Celery peeled, cut large.
2. Mix all the ingredients in the blender until smooth. Serve immediately, sprinkled with watercress.

## Smoothies With Raspberries And Orange

**Ingredients:**

- Malina - 1 tbsp.
- Banana - 4 pcs. ripe
- Red orange - 1 pc.
- Popcorn from movie

**Preparation:**

1. Banana peeled. Three of them are mixed with raspberries until smooth. One banana is mixed with the pulp of a red orange.
2. Lay out the raspberry mixture, on top of the orange and sprinkle the movie.

# Yogurt With Rhubarb

**Ingredients:**

- Rhubarb - 2 stems
- Banana - 1 pc. very ripe
- Yoghurt - 200 ml

**Preparation:**

1. Banana, rhubarb clean, cut into slices. Rhubarb slightly pour water and cook over low heat until softening, about 5 minutes. Cool it down.
2. Beat the rhubarb, bananas and yogurt until smooth.

## Smoothies With Strawberries And Rhubarb

**Ingredients:**

- Rhubarb - 2 stems
- Spinach - a bunch
- Strawberries - 6 pcs.
- Lemon or lime - 1 tbsp.
- Coconut water or water - 1 tbsp.
- Apple green - 1 pc.

**Preparation:**

1. Fruits cleaned, chopped. Mix all ingredients until smooth. Spinach can be used frozen.

# Pumpkin With Cinnamon

**Ingredients:**

- Pumpkin flesh - 400 g.
- Grapefruit - 0,5 pcs.
- Lemon - 0,5 pcs.
- Ground cinnamon - 1 tsp.
- Honey - 2 tsp.

**Preparation:**

1. Pre-prepared (steamed) pumpkin cut into small cubes.
2. Citrus peel and divide into slices.
3. Load the prepared ingredients into the blender bowl, send honey and cinnamon to the bowl.
4. Grind the contents of the blender bowl to a puree state.

# Pumpkin With Oat Flakes

**Ingredients:**

- Pumpkin flesh - 300 g.
- Oat flakes - 3 tbsp. l.
- Honey - 1 tsp.
- Milk - 200 ml.

**Preparation:**

1. Steamed pumpkin cut into small pieces and sent to a bowl blender.
2. Top with oatmeal and add honey.
3. All pour the milk and turn on the blender for a while until the consistency is homogeneous.

# Pumpkin With Spices

**Ingredients:**

- Pumpkin flesh - 400 g.
- Banana - 1 pc.
- Mixture of spices (cinnamon, cloves, nutmeg, dried ginger) - 1 tsp.
- Honey - 1 tsp.
- Vanilla is a pinch.

**Preparation:**

1. Pumpkin and banana cut into cubes and put in a bowl blender.
2. Spice the beans into powder and add them to the hard ingredients.
3. Add honey and vanilla.
4. Beat all blender until homogeneity.

# Carrot With Spinach

**Ingredients:**

- Carrots - 2 pcs.
- Mango - 0.5 pcs.
- Spinach - 2 bunches.
- Water - 120 ml.

**Preparation:**

1. Prepare carrots: remove the top layer from the fruit, peeled carrots on a grater.
2. With half the mango, peel and cut the flesh into small pieces.
3. Spinach thoroughly and wipe with a tissue.
4. All the prepared components should be placed in the blender bowl, filled with water and ground to a homogeneous mass.

# Carrots With Parsley

**Ingredients:**

- Carrots - 1 pc.
- Apple - 1 pc.
- Parsley is a bunch.
- Lettuce leaves - 2-3 pcs.

**Preparation:**

1. Remove the carrots from the top layer and cut into small pieces.
2. With the apple peel and remove the seed box, also cut into pieces.
3. Parsley and salad to wash and dry with a napkin.
4. Put all the ingredients in the bowl of the blender and grind it.

# Carrots With Celery

**Ingredients:**

- Carrots - 2 pcs.
- Tomato - 1 pc.
- Stalk of celery - 2 pcs.
- Salt, pepper - to taste.
- Olive oil - 1 tsp.

**Preparation:**

1. Carrots wash, remove the top layer from it, grate the fruit on the grater.
2. With a tomato peel off. To do this, it will need to be burned with boiling water, so the peel will be removed easily.
3. Stem celery wash, remove from them coarse fibers, cut into pieces.
4. Fold the ingredients in a blender bowl, add butter, spices and beat until smooth.

## Creamy Smoothies With Nuts And Dried Fruits

**Ingredients:**

- ½ cup of natural creamy vanilla yogurt;
- a handful of raisins "kishmish";
- dried apricots - 3-4 pieces;
- prunes - 2-3 pieces;
- a handful of any favorite nuts;
- ice - 4-5 cubes.

**Preparation:**

1. Mix all components with a blender until a uniform thick foam is obtained. To serve a drink, decorating with a sprig of mint or a slice of lemon.

# Cocktail "Good Health"

**Ingredients:**

- ½ green apple;
- 1 stalk of celery;
- ½ avocado pulp;
- 1/3 cup of lime juice;
- sprig of thyme.

**Preparation:**

1. Apple and celery grate. Avocado pulp wipe through a sieve or also pass through a grater.
2. Mix all ingredients with lime juice and pour into a container with a lid.
3. Shake it vigorously and pour over a serving glass. Ready to serve the product decorating a sprig of thyme.

## Detox Smoothies With Strawberries And Beets

**Ingredients:**

- Water - 1 tbsp. (or coconut water)
- Strawberry - 1 tbsp. (can be frozen)
- Avocado - 1/2 pcs.
- Beets - 1/2 tbsp.
- Apple - 1 pc.
- Lemon juice - 1 tbsp.

**Preparation:**

1. Peel the beet and apple, cut into large pieces. Beat all ingredients until smooth.

# Slick Smoothie With Kiwi And Celery

**Ingredients:**

- Celery - 4 stems
- Kiwi - 6-8 pieces.
- Millet flakes - ½ tbsp.
- Salt, cinnamon, lemon juice - to taste
- Honey or maple syrup
- Watercress

**Preparation:**

1. Kiwis cleaned. Millet flakes boil with boiling water until thick porridge. Celery peeled, cut large.
2. Mix all the ingredients in the blender until smooth. Serve immediately, sprinkled with watercress.

# Smoothies With Raspberries And Orange

**Ingredients:**

- Malina - 1 tbsp.
- Banana - 4 pcs. ripe
- Red orange - 1 pc.
- Popcorn from movie

**Preparation:**

1. Banana peeled. Three of them are mixed with raspberries until smooth. One banana is mixed with the pulp of a red orange. Lay out the raspberry mixture, on top of the orange and sprinkle the movie.

# Yogurt With Rhubarb

**Ingredients:**

- Rhubarb - 2 stems
- Banana - 1 pc. very ripe
- Yoghurt - 200 ml

**Preparation:**

1. Banana, rhubarb clean, cut into slices. Rhubarb slightly pour water and cook over low heat until softening, about 5 minutes. Cool it down. Beat the rhubarb, bananas and yogurt until smooth.

## Smoothies With Strawberries And Rhubarb

**Ingredients:**

- Rhubarb - 2 stems
- Spinach - a bunch
- Strawberries - 6 pcs.
- Lemon or lime - 1 tbsp.
- Coconut water or water - 1 tbsp.
- Apple green - 1 pc.

**Preparation:**

1. Fruits cleaned, chopped. Mix all ingredients until smooth. Spinach can be used frozen.

# Pumpkin With Cinnamon

**Ingredients:**

- Pumpkin flesh - 400 g.
- Grapefruit - 0,5 pcs.
- Lemon - 0,5 pcs.
- Ground cinnamon - 1 tsp.
- Honey - 2 tsp.

**Preparation:**

1. Pre-prepared (steamed) pumpkin cut into small cubes.
2. Citrus peel and divide into slices.
3. Load the prepared ingredients into the blender bowl, send honey and cinnamon to the bowl.
4. Grind the contents of the blender bowl to a puree state.

# Pumpkin With Oat Flakes

**Ingredients:**

- Pumpkin flesh - 300 g.
- Oat flakes - 3 tbsp. l.
- Honey - 1 tsp.
- Milk - 200 ml.

**Preparation:**

1. Steamed pumpkin cut into small pieces and sent to a bowl blender.
2. Top with oatmeal and add honey.
3. All pour the milk and turn on the blender for a while until the consistency is homogeneous.

# Pumpkin With Spices

**Ingredients:**

- Pumpkin flesh - 400 g.
- Banana - 1 pc.
- Mixture of spices (cinnamon, cloves, nutmeg, dried ginger) - 1 tsp.
- Honey - 1 tsp.
- Vanilla is a pinch.

**Preparation:**

1. Pumpkin and banana cut into cubes and put in a bowl blender.
2. Spice the beans into powder and add them to the hard ingredients.
3. Add honey and vanilla.
4. Beat all blender until homogeneity.

# Carrot With Spinach

**Ingredients:**

- Carrots - 2 pcs.
- Mango - 0.5 pcs.
- Spinach - 2 bunches.
- Water - 120 ml.

**Preparation:**

1. Prepare carrots: remove the top layer from the fruit, peeled carrots on a grater.
2. With half the mango, peel and cut the flesh into small pieces.
3. Spinach thoroughly and wipe with a tissue.
4. All the prepared components should be placed in the blender bowl, filled with water and ground to a homogeneous mass.

# Carrots With Parsley

**Ingredients:**

- Carrots - 1 pc.
- Apple - 1 pc.
- Parsley is a bunch.
- Lettuce leaves - 2-3 pcs.

**Preparation:**

1. Remove the carrots from the top layer and cut into small pieces.
2. With the apple peel and remove the seed box, also cut into pieces.
3. Parsley and salad to wash and dry with a napkin.
4. Put all the ingredients in the bowl of the blender and grind it.

# Carrots With Celery

**Ingredients:**

- Carrots - 2 pcs.
- Tomato - 1 pc.
- Stalk of celery - 2 pcs.
- Salt, pepper - to taste.
- Olive oil - 1 tsp.

**Preparation:**

1. Carrots wash, remove the top layer from it, grate the fruit on the grater.
2. With a tomato peel off. To do this, it will need to be burned with boiling water, so the peel will be removed easily.
3. Stem celery wash, remove from them coarse fibers, cut into pieces.
4. Fold the ingredients in a blender bowl, add butter, spices and beat until smooth.

## Creamy Smoothies With Nuts And Dried Fruits
**Ingredients:**

- ½ cup of natural creamy vanilla yogurt;
- a handful of raisins "kishmish";
- dried apricots - 3-4 pieces;
- prunes - 2-3 pieces;
- a handful of any favorite nuts;
- ice - 4-5 cubes.

**Preparation:**

1. Mix all components with a blender until a uniform thick foam is obtained. To serve a drink, decorating with a sprig of mint or a slice of lemon.

# Cocktail "Good Health"

**Ingredients:**

- ½ green apple;
- 1 stalk of celery;
- ½ avocado pulp;
- 1/3 cup of lime juice;
- sprig of thyme.

**Preparation:**

1. Apple and celery grate. Avocado pulp wipe through a sieve or also pass through a grater. Mix all ingredients with lime juice and pour into a container with a lid. Shake it vigorously and pour over a serving glass. Ready to serve the product decorating a sprig of thyme.

# Oatmeal Smoothies

**Ingredients:**

- Milk - 1 tbsp.
- Oat flakes - 2 tbsp. (quickly brewed or brewed in advance)
- Banana - 1 pc.
- Honey - 1 tbsp.

**Preparation:**

1. In the blender, pour the milk, cut into banana slices, add oat flakes and honey. Mix everything until smooth.

# November Smoothies With Persimmons

**Ingredients:**

- Persimmon - 3 pcs.
- Orange - 1 pc. (or a pair of mandarins)
- Dried apricots - 10-12 pcs.
- Mango - 1 pc. (can be replaced with papaya, apple or pumpkin)
- Orange juice, cold green tea or water
- Maple syrup or honey
- Cinnamon - if desired

**Preparation:**

1. Clear fruits from the peel and bones, partitions. Mix in a blender to taste.

# Mandarin Smoothies

**Ingredients:**

- Mandarin - 2 pcs.
- Frozen banana - 1 pc.
- Vegetable milk - 1 tbsp.
- Honey - 1 tsp.
- Vanillin - to taste

**Preparation:**

1. Peel the banana, cut into small pieces and send to the freezer for 20 minutes. Clear the tangerines from the peel and bones. Load all components into the blender and beat.

# Grape And Cherry Smoothies

**Ingredients:**

- Red grapes - 150 g (pitted)
- Frozen cherries - 100 g
- Mint leaves
- Dates - 3 pcs.
- Water - 100-150 ml

**Preparation:**

1. Separate the bones from the dates. Beat all ingredients until smooth.

# Mango-Pineapple Smoothies

**Ingredients:**

- Banana - 1 pc.
- Mango - 1 pc.
- Pineapple - 100 g
- Apple - 1 pc.
- Water - to taste

**Preparation:**

1. Peel the fruit, cut it large and load into a bowl, whip until smooth, adding water to the required density.

# Blueberry-Buckwheat Smoothies

**Ingredients:**

- Blueberries - 100 g (fresh or frozen)
- Buckwheat - 4 tbsp. l.
- Banana - 1 pc.
- Dates - 2-4 pcs.
- Water - 150 ml.

**Preparation:**

1. Buckwheat germ. Banana cleaned, the dates separated bones. Load into a blender and whisk until smooth.

# Sea-Buckthorn-Calyon Smoothies

**Ingredients:**

- Kalina - 2 bunches
- Sea-buckthorn - 3 tablespoons
- Banana - 1 pc. (can be frozen)
- Honey - 1 tbsp. or dates, agave / Jerusalem artichoke syrup
- Vegetable milk - 50 ml or water

**Preparation:**

1. Kalina and sea-buckthorn rub through a sieve. Beat with honey and vegetable milk, add a banana and beat again.

## Pomegranate Smoothies With Orange

**Ingredients:**

- Pomegranate - 1 pc.
- Orange - 2 pcs.
- Water

**Preparation:**

1. Squeeze orange juice. Separate pomegranate seeds, load them into a blender, add orange fresh, drinking water at will and whip.
2. Strain through gauze, strainer or special pouch.

# Cranberry Smoothies

**Ingredients:**

- Sesame seeds - 60 g
- Cranberries - 120 g of cranberries (can be frozen)
- Banana - 1 pc.
- Water - 300 ml
- Honey, syrup - to taste

**Preparation:**

1. First you need to make sesame milk: put the sesame into a blender, pour water, whisk thoroughly. Strain the milk through a gauze or fine sieve and pour it back into the blender.
2. Add cranberries to the milk (you can not defrost, then the cocktail will turn out slightly cool), a banana and a sweetener. All thoroughly beat, and our vitamin cocktail is ready!

# Beetroot Latte

**Ingredients:**

- Vegetable milk - 1 ¼ tbsp.
- Beet - 1 pc. mean
- Cinnamon - ¼ tsp
- The root of ginger - 1 tsp. (grated)
- Vanilla, syrup or honey - to taste

**Preparation:**

1. Prepare the beets, peel, beat with vegetable milk in a blender until smooth. Add cinnamon, ginger and beat again.
2. Strain the mixture through a fine sieve or gauze, and then pour into a small saucepan and heat, but do not boil. Remove from heat, add vanilla and syrup.

## Cedar Smoothies With Cherries And Chocolate

**Ingredients:**

- Cedar milk - 400 ml
- Cherry (frozen) - 200 g
- Chocolate (finely chopped) - 30 g
- Syrup (maple) - 2 tbsp. l.
- Mint - 2-3 leaves

**Preparation:**

1. Mix all ingredients in a blender until smooth.

# Sesame-orange milkshake

**Ingredients:**

- Sesame - 1/2 tbsp.
- Water - 2 tbsp.
- Orange - 2 pcs.
- The dates Caspian - 8 pcs.
- Cinnamon - to taste

**Preparation:**

1. Soak sesame overnight. Rinse well, load into a blender, add water and beat until smooth. Squeeze sesame milk through a cheesecloth or synthetic pouch.
2. Oranges cleaned of peel, seeds and partitions. Finike soak in hot water and peel hard skin and bones.
3. In a clean blender, load jelly, dates, oranges, cinnamon and beat until smooth.

## Sesame Smoothies With Berries

**Ingredients:**

- Sesame white - 1/2 tbsp.
- Banana - 1 pc. (very ripe)
- Water - 2 tbsp.
- Berries - 1/2 tbsp. (currant, raspberry, strawberry)

**Preparation:**

1. Soak sesame overnight. Rinse, put in a blender. Add water, fresh or frozen berries and whisk until smooth. To taste, you can add a sweetener.

## Smoothie Recipe

### 1: The Green Mango Booster

Ingredients
11/4 cups unsweetened almond milk
2 cups baby spinach
1 cup frozen mango
1 frozen banana
1 teaspoon bee pollen
2 teaspoons spirulina
4 tablespoons (1 scoop) protein powder

Instructions
Add ingredients into a blender and blend until smooth.

## 2: Berry Orange Creamsicle Smoothie

Ingredients
1 frozen banana
1 cup of blueberries
1 orange, peeled and chopped into pieces
1/4 cup rolled oats
1/3 cup low-fat greek yoghurt

Instructions
Place all ingredients in a blender and blend until smooth.

Pour into a glass or shaker and enjoy! If you smoothie is a little too thick, add a few ice cubes.

## 3. Strawberry Banana Protein Blast

Ingredients
1 frozen banana
1 cup milk of choice
1/2 cup chopped strawberries
1/4 cup low-fat greek yoghurt
1 tbsp peanut butter

Instructions
Blend all ingredients together until smooth.

## 4. Fruity Spinach Green Smoothie

Ingredients
1/2 cup blueberries
1 tbsp almond butter
1/2 cup Greek yogurt
1/2 medium banana, sliced
1 medium peach, pitted
1 cup spinach
Water to fill line

Instructions
Add all ingredients to your large nutribullet cup, saving water for last.

Once you have filled the cup with water to the fill line, puree ingredients to desired consistency.

## 5. Post Workout Melon Berry Smoothie

Ingredients

1 cup strawberries

1 cup watermelon

1 cup cantaloupe

1 packet of Emergen-C tangerine flavor (or flavor of choice)

4-5 ice cubes

Water to the fill line (or 1 cup)

Instructions

Place ingredients in the Nutribullet or blender.

Add water to the fill line (or 1 cup water).

Blend until frothy.

Garnish with fresh strawberries.

## 6. Blueberry Power Smoothie

Ingredients
1 cup Silk Light Original Soymilk
1/2 cup frozen wild blueberries
1/2 frozen banana
1/4 small avocado
1 cup Earthbound Farm power greens
1 scoop vanilla whey protein
Water
1/8 tsp turmeric, if desired
1-2 Tbsp unsweetened cocoa powder, if desired
Stevia, if desired

Instructions
Blend all ingredients until smooth and creamy.

Add water to reach desired consistency.

## 7. Kale, Berry And Acai Power Smoothie

Ingredients

1 ripe banana

1/3 of a cup of blueberries

1/3 of a cup of strawberries

1/2 a cup of kale leaves (remove the hard parts of the stalks)

1/4 of a cup of almond milk or water

1 tablespoon of ground flax seed

1 tablespoon of hemp powder

1 tablespoon of chia seeds

1 tablespoon of acai

1 teaspoon of cinnamon

Instructions

Place all the ingredients in a blender together, removing the banana from the peel first, then blend into a delicious mix. Depending how liquid you like your smoothie, you may want to add a little more water.

## 8. Cherry Bakewell Protein Smoothie

Ingredients
1 cup frozen cherries
1 banana, fresh or frozen
1 tbsp almond butter
1 cup unsweetened almond milk (or milk of choice)
1 tbsp chia seeds
1 tbsp milled/ground flaxseed

Optional add ins
1.5 tsps maca powder
Handful of greens (spinach/kale etc)

Instructions
Add all the ingredients to a blender or smoothie maker and blend until smooth.
Serve immediately.

## 9. Green Warrior Protein Smoothie

Ingredients

1/2 cup (125 mL) fresh red grapefruit juice
1 cup (25 g) destemmed dinosaur/lacinato kale or baby spinach
1 large sweet apple (200 g), cored and roughly chopped
1 cup (130 g) chopped cucumber
1 medium/large stalk celery (85 g), chopped (about 3/4 cup)
3 to 4 tablespoons (30 to 40 g) hemp hearts, to taste
1/3 cup (55 g) frozen mango
2 tablespoons (4 g) packed fresh mint leaves
1 1/2 teaspoons virgin coconut oil (optional)
4 ice cubes, or as needed

Instructions

Juice a red grapefruit and add 1/2 cup grapefruit juice to the blender.

Now add the kale (or spinach), apple, cucumber, celery, hemp, mango, mint, coconut oil (if using), and ice. Blend on high until super smooth. (If using a Vitamix, use the tamper stick to push it down until it blends). You can add a bit of water if necessary to get it blending.

Pour into a glass and enjoy immediately!

## 10. Raw Caramel Apple Smoothie (Vegan, Gluten Free)

Ingredients
1.5 cups fresh raw coconut water
scant 1 cup raw coconut meat
2 tablespoons unsalted almond butter
1/2 apple cored and chopped roughly
4 dates
1/3 cup cashews
tiny splash vanilla extract or pinch vanilla bean powder
**optional:** 1 teaspoon maca and/or 1 teaspoon lucuma

Instructions
In the bowl of a high powered blender, combine all of the ingredients: raw coconut water, raw coconut meat, almond butter, apple, dates, cashews, vanilla extract and (optionally) maca and/or lucuma.

Blend on high until the smoothie is creamy.
Serve immediately.

## 11. Grapefruit Ginger Citrus Green Smoothie

Ingredients
1 c water
2" chunk fresh ginger
1/4-1/2 medium cucumber, sliced
1 c spinach
1/4-1/2 medium grapefruit
1 tbsp tahini
1/2 lemon, juice of
1/2 c ice

optional:
1 scoop protein {vega protein + greens natural flavor}
ginger kombucha
collegen

Instructions
Place all ingredients in a high-speed blender and blend until smooth.

## 12. Creamy Turmeric Smoothie

Ingredients
1 Cup Frozen Pineapple
1/2 Frozen Banana
1/2 Inch Fresh Ginger, Grated
3/4 Cup Chai Tea Concentrate (or sub strong brewed Chai tea)
1/2 Cup Almond or Coconut Milk
Juice of 1/2 Lime
1/4 Teaspoon Ground Turmeric
**Optional:** Coconut Flakes for Garnish

Instructions
Combine all ingredients in a blender, and blend until smooth.
If the mixture is too thick, add a bit more almond milk.
Garnish with coconut flakes.

## 13. Banana Coconut Cream

Ingredients
1 1/2 cup of plain greek yogurt
2 bananas
1 cup canned coconut milk
1 tbsp agave syrup – optional

Instructions
Combine all ingredients in blender.

Blend until smooth.

## 14. Walnut Pineapple Workout Replenisher

Ingredients
2 tablespoons walnuts
1/2 cup organic black beans
1/2 cup organic baby spinach
2/3 cup So Delicious Greek Style Cultured Coconut Milk Yogurt
1 cup frozen pineapple
1 banana
1 cup assorted berries
1-2 cups coconut water (depending on desired consistency)

Instructions
Combine and mix in a blender for 30 seconds, or until smooth.

## 15. Blueberry Avocado And Spinach Smoothie

Ingredients
1 cup blueberries, frozen or fresh
1 cup fresh spinach leaves
1 cup almond-coconut milk (you can use just coconut or just almond)
1/2 ripe avocado, skinned and pitted
1 tablespoon chia seeds
1/4 teaspoon cinnamon
1 tablespoon honey
1 scoop protein powder (optional)
1/2 fresh ice

Instructions
Place all ingredients in blender and puree.

Serve in glass.

Add a few fresh blueberries (optional).

# Smoothies For Weight Loss

**1. Berry Oat Breakfast Smoothie**

Ingredients
1/2 cup old fashioned rolled oats
1 cup milk (more as needed)
1/2 cup frozen berries
3 tablespoons honey (or to taste)
1/3 cup vanilla yogurt or greek yogurt
1/4 cup ice

Instructions
Add all ingredients to a blender.
Cover tightly and pulse until ice is broken up, then puree until smooth.
Taste and add sweeter if needed or milk if it is too thick.
Serve immediately.

## 2. Chocolate Peanut Butter Banana Breakfast Smoothie

Ingredients
2 large overripe bananas, peeled, sliced and frozen*
1 cup original almond milk (or more to thin as desired)
3/4 cup ice
1/4 cup creamy peanut butter
2 Tbsp unsweetened cocoa powder
1/2 tsp vanilla extract

Instructions
Add all ingredients to a blender a process until well pureed. Serve immediately.
*The overripe bananas will add the sweetness for the smoothie so use some that have a generous amount of speckles, don't use black bananas though those are just gross.

### 3. Green Breakfast Blast

Ingredients
1/2 Cup Spinach
1/2 Cup Kale
1 Kiwi
1/4 Cup Greek Yogurt
1 Banana
10 Grapes
1 Chunk Cucumber
1/2 Stalk Celery
1/2 Apple
1 1/2 Cups Water

Instructions
Add all ingredients into your Tall Cup and extract for 30 seconds, or until smooth.

Serve.

## 4. Spinach And Avocado Smoothie

Ingredients
1 avocado, pitted
1 cup fresh spinach
1 large ripe banana
1 tablespoon natural peanut butter
1 cup milk
Handful of ice cubes

Instructions
Blend all ingredients in a blender on high speed until very smooth.

## 5. Chocolate Chia Cherry Smoothie

Ingredients
1 cup unsweetened nut, soy, or cow's milk
2 tablespoons chia seeds
1 tablespoon unsweetened cocoa powder
2 cups pitted, halved cherries
1 medium-size ripe banana
4 to 5 ice cubes

Instructions
Combine ingredients in the order listed in a blender. Blend on high speed until everything is smooth.

## 6. Banana And Coconut Water

Ingredients
1/2 banana, chopped and frozen
1/4 ripe avocado, pitted
1 small handful spinach
1 handful frozen berries
1 1/2 teaspoons shelled hemp seeds
1/4 teaspoon wheatgrass powder
1/4 cucumber, chopped
1 tablespoon raw cacao nibs
Scant 1 cup coconut water or water, plus extra if needed

Instructions
Chop banana and place in a freezer bag.

Seal and freeze overnight until solid.

Put banana in blender with remaining ingredients.

Blend until smooth and creamy, adding a little more water if necessary.

## 7. Carrot Cake Smoothie (Gluten-Free + Vegan)

Ingredients
1 cup carrots, peeled and then grated
1 organic banana, frozen
1 1/2 cups homemade almond milk (or other non-dairy milk of your choice)
1/4 cup raw unsalted cashews, soaked for two hours (or 1/4 cup homemade cashew nut butter)
1 teaspoon vanilla extract
1 Medjool date
1 tablespoon organic raw shelled hemp seeds
1/2 teaspoon ground cinnamon
1/4 teaspoon ground ginger or 1 teaspoon grated fresh ginger
1/8 teaspoon ground nutmeg
1/8 teaspoon ground cloves

Optional – instead of the hemp seeds, for additional nutritional support, you could also opt for a scoop of Vega Plant-Based Protein Powder, either the Vanilla Chai or straight Vanilla would be great.

Instructions
Add all of the ingredients to your high speed blender and process until smooth and creamy.
Top with a little cinnamon and a pinch of grated carrots.
Enjoy immediately.

## 8. Red Velvet Beet Smoothie

Ingredients
1 medium red beet, raw, peeled and chopped
About 4 large strawberries (I used frozen)
1 overripe banana, frozen
2 Tbsp cocoa powder
1/8 tsp + 9 drops liquid stevia (or 3 dates, pitted)
1/2 cup plain greek yogurt (Chobani is my favorite)
1/4-1/2 cup water

Instructions
In a high powered blender, combine all of the ingredients (using only 1/4 cup of water to start).

Blend until smooth.

Add 1/4 cup more water to thin, if necessary, to reach desired consistency. Enjoy!

## 9. Kiwi Green Smoothie

Ingredients
2 frozen bananas
1 fresh kiwi, skin removed
1 cup water
2 handfuls baby spinach

Instructions
Place all ingredients in a blender and blend until smooth.

## 10. Anti-Inflammatory Green Smoothie With Turmeric

Ingredients
1 cup frozen or fresh pineapple chunks
1 handful of arugula
1 handful of spinach and kale
1/2 inch fresh ginger root, peeled
1 1/2 cups of coconut water and/or green tea
1/2 tsp. of ground turmeric powder or 1/2 inch fresh turmeric root
1/2 tsp. ground cinnamon

*optional scoop vegan and gluten-free protein powder water and ice to blend.

Instructions
Blend ingredients.

Top it with chia seeds and a handful of walnuts.

Enjoy!

## 11. Strawberry, Banana And Green Tea Smoothie

Ingredients

2 cups Fresh Strawberries, washed

1 medium Banana, frozen

1/2 cup Greek Yogurt

1/2 cup Green Tea, chilled (made with 1 tea bags or 1 tsp of loose tea)

4 tbsp Flax seed

2 tbsp Honey

Instructions

Place all the ingredients in a blender and blend until smooth.

Pour into a glass and serve immediately.

## 12. Peanut Butter Smoothie

Ingredients
1 Small banana
1/2 cup Low-fat peanut butter
1/2 cup Low-fat milk
1 spoon Chocolate whey protein
6 Ice cubes

Instructions
Blend all the ingredients well and your fat-burning smoothie is ready.

## 13. Mango Smoothie

Ingredients
1/2 cup Mango cubes
1 tablespoon Sugar
2 tablespoons Fat-free yogurt
6 Ice cubes

Instructions
Blend everything together.
Your summer mango smoothie is ready to serve. This smoothie has only 298 calories.

## 14. Almond Orange Smoothie

Ingredients

1 cup (250 mL) vanilla-flavoured almond beverage
1/2 cup (125 mL) orange juice
Juice from one lemon
Juice from one lime
Handful of ice
1 Tbsp (15 mL) honey

Instructions
Blend all ingredients together.

## 15. C-Blast Smoothie

Ingredients

1 large pink grapefruit, peeled, seeded and cut into chunks

1/2 cup (125 mL) crushed pineapple, canned or fresh

1/2 cup (125 mL) fresh or frozen strawberries (if using fresh, add 1/4 cup [60 mL] ice for extra froth)

1/2 cup (125 mL) non-fat Greek yogurt

Instructions

Blend all ingredients together.

## 16. Strawberry Chia Watermelon Smoothie

Ingredients

1 1/2 cups (240 g) fresh watermelon, cubed (black seeds removed)

1 cup (120 g) frozen strawberries

1/2 ripe banana (50 g), previously peeled, chopped and frozen

1/2 - 3/4 cup (120-180 ml) unsweetened plain almond milk

1 lime, juiced (~30 ml)

1 Tbsp chia or hemp seeds (optional)

Instructions

Add all ingredients to a blender and blend until creamy and smooth, adding more almond milk to thin, or more frozen strawberries or ice to thicken.

Taste and adjust seasonings as needed, adding more lime for acidity, banana for sweetness, or watermelon for a more intense watermelon flavor.

Serves 2 - top with additional chia seeds to mock watermelon seeds! Best when fresh, though leftovers keep covered in the refrigerator for 1-2 days.

## 17. Banana Ginger Smoothie

Ingredients
2 tbsp ground flaxseeds
1 cup frozen blueberries
1 frozen banana
1 tbsp fresh grated ginger
Handful baby spinach
12-16 oz water
Ice (optional, for consistency)

Instructions
Combine all ingredients in a blender and blend to perfection.

## 18. Mocha Smoothie

Ingredients

1/2 cup vanilla frozen yogurt

1 shot espresso

2 teaspoons raw cocoa

Instructions

Combine all ingredients in a blender and blend to perfection.

## 19. Mulberry, Lavender, And Kale Energizing Smoothie

Ingredients
1 frozen banana
1 cup fresh mulberries (or 1/2 cup dried)
1 cup kale
1 tablespoon dried lavender
1 cups apple juice
1/2 cup rolled oats
1/4 cup raw cashews
1 teaspoon lucuma powder
1 teaspoon vanilla extract

Instructions
Add all ingredients to the blender and blend until smooth.
The lavender complements the mulberries beautifully and adds a calm edge to the energizing kale, berries, cashews, and oats.

## 20. Orange Papaya Passion Fruit

Ingredients
1/2 cup of water
1 orange
1/2 lime
1 medium papaya
1 passion fruit

Instructions
Juice the orange and lime.
Place papaya (deseeded and chopped), water, passion fruit and juice in blender.
Blend together until smooth.

## 21. Spicy Grapefruit Pineapple

Ingredients
2 grapefruits
1/2 pineapple
1/4 inch of gingerroot
5 ice cubes
Water to make it blend

Instructions
Place all ingredients in a blender and process until smooth.
Serve immediately.

# Banana Auburn Smoothie

INGREDIENTS

- 1 sliced banana
- ¾ cup Vanilla Yogurt
- 1 tablespoon honey
- ½ teaspoon freshly grated ginger

INSTRUCTIONS

Combine all ingredients and blend till smooth. Best for soothing nausea, heartburn, digestion and other tummy discomfort, this is a natural medicine drink for two people.

Each glass contains:

Calories – 157

Fat - 1 gram

Saturated fat - 0.8 gram

Sodium - 57 mg

Carbs - 34 grams

Sugars - 28 grams

Fiber - 1.5 grams

Protein - 5 grams

## Orange Dream

INGREDIENTS

1 peeled navel orange

¼ cup nonfat yogurt

2 tablespoons ice-covered orange concentrate

¼ teaspoon vanilla extract

4 ice cubes

INSTRUCTIONS

Combine and process till smooth. This low calorie, citrus-infused drink is perfect for cooling down following a hard workout or after a warm day by the sea.

Each glass contains:

Calories – 160

Protein - 3 grams

Carbs - 36 grams

Fiber - 3 grams

Sugars - 28 grams

Fat - 1 gram

Saturated fat - 0.5 gram

Sodium - 60 mg

## Green Blueberry Banana Drink

INGREDIENTS

- 3 tablespoons water
- 1 green tea bag
- 2 teaspoons honey
- 1½ cup frozen blueberries
- ½ medium Banana
- ¾ cups calcium fortified light vanilla soy milk

INSTRUCTIONS

Microwave water at high temperature until it steams in a little bowl. Add the tea bag and allow brewing for three minutes before removing the tea bag. Stir in honey in the tea till it melts away. Combine it with the milk, banana and berries in a whizzer with ice squashing ability.

Blend on the highest adjustment or ice press until even. Add extra water if your blender so requires for processing. Pour the smoothie in a tall crystal glass for one person to enjoy.

Each glass contains:

Calories – 269

Fat - 2.5 grams

Saturated fat - 0.2 gram

Sodium - 52 mg

Carbs - 63 grams

Sugars - 38.5 grams

Fiber - 8 grams

Protein - 3.5 grams

## Berry Breakfast

INGREDIENTS

- 1 cup frozen unsweetened raspberries
- ¾ cup cold rice milk or unsweetened almond
- ¼ cup freezing pitted sugar-free raspberries or cherries

- 1½ tablespoons honey
- 2 teaspoons finely grated fresh ginger
- 1 teaspoon ground flaxseed
- 2 teaspoons fresh lemon juice

INSTRUCTIONS

Combine all fixings in a blender and add lemon juice for taste. Puree until smooth and pour into two chilled crystal glasses to start your morning off by an explosion of this fruit-filled, zero-saturated fat smoothie!

Each glass contains:

Calories - 112

Fat - 1.5 grams

Sodium - 56 mg

Carbs - 25.5 grams

Sugars - 20 grams

Fiber - 3 grams

Protein - 1 gram

## Best of the World

INGREDIENTS

- 1 cup plain nonfat yogurt
- 1 banana
- ½ cup orange juice
- 6 frozen strawberries

INSTRUCTIONS

Combine all ingredients and blend for around 20 seconds and then scrape down the flanks. Blend again for a quarter of a minute before serving to one person. Sip this saturated fat-free drink with your breakfast and you will feel full until lunch.

Each glass contains:

Calories – 300

Protein - 14 grams

Carbs - 63 grams

Fiber - 5 grams

Sugars - 45 grams

Fat - 0.5 gram

Sodium - 180 mg

## Pineapple Desire

INGREDIENTS

- 1 cup low-fat or light vanilla yogurt
- 6 ice cubes
- 1 cup pineapple chunks

INSTRUCTIONS

Combine the ice cubes and yogurt, blend, pulsing when needed, till the cubes appear in big chunks. Add the pineapple, blend on "whip" swiftness until even and serve to one person. This extravagantly thick smoothie can equally satisfy your wish for an ice cream!

Each glass contains:

Calories – 283

Fat - 3.5 grams

Saturated fat - 2 grams

Sodium - 167 mg

Carbs - 53.5 grams

Sugars - 48 grams

Fiber - 2 grams

Protein - 13 grams

## Kiwi Strawberry Smoothie

INGREDIENTS

- 1¼ cup cold apple juice
- 1 sliced ripe banana
- 1 sliced kiwi fruit
- 5 frozen strawberries
- 1½ teaspoons honey

INSTRUCTIONS

Combine all ingredients, blend until even and serve to four people. Stay filled and combat disease with this high fibre smoothie. It becomes healthier once you make use of organic kiwis as they contain elevated levels of heart-friendly vitamin C and polyphenols.

Each glass contains:

Calories – 87

Fat - 0.3 gram

Sodium - 3.5 mg

Carbs - 22 grams

Sugars - 16.5 grams

Fiber - 1.5 grams

Protein - 0.5 gram

## BBS Smoothie

INGREDIENTS

- 1¼ cup light soy milk

- ½ cup frozen loose-pack blueberries

- ½ sliced frozen banana

- 2 teaspoons sugar or two packets of artificial sweetener

- 1 teaspoon pure vanilla extract

INSTRUCTIONS

Combine one cup of milk, the banana, blueberries, vanilla extract and sugar or sweetener. Blend for half a minute or till smooth and add the remaining milk or more depending on how thin or thick you desire your smoothie to be. Rest assured that the succulent blueberries will burst its full flavour within this delightful drink for two people.

For a more healthier drink, you may skip the artificial sweetener or sugar as the fruits can already make it effortlessly sweet.

Each glass contains:

Calories – 125

Fat - 1.5 grams

Saturated fat - 0.1 gram

Sodium - 60 mg

Carbs - 25 grams

Sugars - 11 grams

Fiber - 2 grams

Protein - 3 grams

# Tropical Perfection

INGREDIENTS

- 1 papaya, cut into chunks
- 1 cup fat-free plain yogurt
- ½ cup fresh pineapple chunks
- ½ cup crushed ice
- 1 tsp coconut extract
- 1 tsp ground flaxseed

INSTRUCTIONS

Combine all ingredients, process for around half a minute, or till frosty and smooth, and serve. Thick similar to a milkshake, smoothie infused with coconut transports you to a sultry island.

Each glass contains:

Calories – 299

Fat - 1.5 grams

Saturated fat - 0.1 gram

Sodium - 149 mg

Carbs - 64 grams

Sugars - 44 grams

Fiber - 7 grams

Protein - 13 grams

## Simply Peachy

INGREDIENTS

- 1 cup of 1% milk
- 2 tablespoons low fat or nonfat vanilla yogurt
- ½ cup frozen peaches
- ½ cup strawberries
- ⅛ of a teaspoon of powdered ginger

- 2 tsp whey protein powder
- 3 ice cubes

INSTRUCTIONS

Blend together all liquid elements with protein powder to split the gritty powder, besides making sure it is evenly dispersed. Add next the mushy elements, like fruits and pre-cooked oatmeal, and then toss in the ice last. For a denser shake, you could toss inside more ice cubes to add more volume minus the calories. Fat-free vanilla ice cream makes this smoothie slimming and sinful.

Each glass contains:

Calories – 150

Fat - 2 grams

Saturated fat - 1 gram

Sodium - 73 mg

Carbs - 26.5 grams

Sugars - 24 grams

Fiber - 2 grams

Protein - 9 grams

## **Morning Madness**

### INGREDIENTS

- 6 pieces peeled, pitted and sliced apricots
- 2 pieces peeled and chopped ripe mangoes of around 12 ounces each
- 1 cup low-fat milk or basic low-fat yogurt
- 4 tsp fresh lemon juice
- ¼ tsp vanilla extract
- 8 ice cubes
- Lemon peel twists for garnishing

### INSTRUCTIONS

Place the vanilla extract, apricots, lemon juice, mangoes and milk or yogurt in a mixer and process for eight seconds. Add the ice cubes and blend for another eight seconds, or till smooth. Pour into high glasses, enhance with twists of lemon, if preferred and dish out to two people immediately. Fresh lemon juice intensifies the tangy squelch to this sugary smoothie.

Each glass contains:

Calories – 252

Fat - 3.5 grams

Saturated fat - 1.5 grams

Sodium - 57 mg

Carbs - 53 grams

Sugars - 45.5 grams

Fiber - 6 grams

Protein - 7 grams

# Watermelon Miracle

INGREDIENTS

- 2 cups chopped watermelon
- ¼ cup fat-free milk
- 2 cups ice

INSTRUCTIONS

Combine the milk and watermelon, and process for a quarter of a minute, or till smooth. Add the ice and mix for another 20 seconds, or to your preferred consistency. Add extra ice, if wished, and mix for another 10 seconds.

Make sure to buy the seedless watermelon variety when buying the fruit. Otherwise, make sure to remove all the seeds prior to blending.

Each glass contains:

Calories – 56

Fat - 0.3 grams

Sodium - 19.5 mg

Carbs - 13 grams

Sugars - 11 grams

Fiber - 0.5 grams

Protein - 2 grams

## Berry Nice Workout Drink

INGREDIENTS

- 1½ cup chopped strawberries
- 1 cup blueberries
- ½ cup raspberries
- 2 tablespoons honey

- 1 tsp fresh lemon juice
- ½ c ice cubes

## INSTRUCTIONS

Blend all and serve to one person. Get the power you require to drive through your exercise in jiffies with this simple to make smoothie.

Each glass contains:

Calories - 162

Fat - 1 gram

Saturated fat - 0.1 gram

Sodium - 5 mg

Carbs - 41.5 grams

Sugars - 32 grams

Fiber - 6 grams

Protein - 2 grams

## Sunrise Drink

INGREDIENTS

- 1 banana
- 1 cup chilled apricot nectar
- 1 container of 8 ounces low-fat peach yogurt
- 1 tablespoon frozen lemonade essence or concentrate
- Half cup chilled club soda

INGREDIENTS

Combine the lemonade concentrate, banana, yogurt and apricot nectar, and process for half a minute, or till creamy and smooth. Stir in the club soda before immediate serving to four people. This blended peach and apricot smoothie would look like a sunrise to start your day right.

Each glass contains:

Calories – 130

Fat - 0.5 gram

Saturated fat - 0.5 gram

Sodium - 43.5 mg

Carbs - 29 grams

Sugars - 16 grams

Fiber - 1.5 grams

Protein - 2.5 grams

## Berry Plain Sensation

INGREDIENTS

- ½ cup frozen unsweetened raspberries

- ½ cup frozen unsweetened strawberries
- ¾ cup unsweetened pineapple juice
- 1 cup fat-free vanilla yogurt

INSTRUCTIONS

Combine all ingredients, blend until even and serve to two people. Fat-free plain yogurt sugarcoats this tasty fruit drink.

Each glass contains:

Calories – 192

Fat - 0.5 gram

Saturated fat - 0.1 gram

Sodium - 86.5 mg

Carbs - 41 grams

Sugars - 35 grams

Fiber - 2.5 grams

Protein - 7 grams

## Tutti Frutti

INGREDIENTS

- ½ cup loosely packed mixed frozen berries or strawberries

- ½ cup canned crush pineapple in juice

- ½ cup plain yogurt

- ½ cup sliced ripe banana

- ½ cup orange juice

INSTRUCTIONS

Combine all ingredients in a blender fitted using the metallic blade making sure to include the juice with the crushed pineapple. Process for around two minutes, or till smooth, and serve to two people. A squish of orange sap infuses seasonal citrus hooked on this healthful and cool snack.

Each glass contains:

Calories – 140

Fat - 2.5 grams

Saturated fat - 1.5 grams

Sodium - 30 mg

Carbs - 29 grams

Sugars - 16 grams

Fiber - 2.5 grams

Protein - 3.5 grams

## Luscious Smoothie

INGREDIENTS

- 1 cup skim milk
- 1 cup frozen and unsweetened strawberries
- 1 tablespoon cold-pressed organic flax seed oil

- 1 tablespoon sunflower or pumpkin seeds (optional)

## INSTRUCTIONS

Mix frozen strawberries and milk in a food processor and blend for a minute. Transfer the mixture into a crystal glass, besides stirring in the flax seed oil. You may also serve it with a tablespoon of pumpkin or sunflower seeds.

Each glass contains:

Calories – 256

Fat - 14 grams

Saturated fat - 1.5 grams

Sodium - 106 mg

Carbs - 26 grams

Sugars - 19 grams

Fiber - 3 grams

Protein - 9 grams

## Slim Down Smoothie

INGREDIENTS

- 1 cup frozen blueberries, raspberries or strawberries

- ½ cup low-fat yogurt of any flavor

- ½ cup orange juice or any other juice

INSTRUCTIONS

Place all ingredients in a food processor and beat for half a minute. Then blend for another half minute, or till smooth. Wonderfully profuse and delicious, this smoothie easily alternates for ice cream and milkshakes. This recipe is good for one person.

Each glass contains:

Calories – 185

Fat - 2 grams

Saturated fat - 1 gram

Sodium - 90 mg

Carbs - 35 grams

Sugars - 26 grams

Fiber - 3.5 grams

Protein - 8 grams

## Noble Soy Smoothie

INGREDIENTS

- 1 cup vanilla soy milk fortified by calcium
- ½ cup frozen blueberries
- ½ cup corn flakes cereal
- 1 sliced frozen banana

## INSTRUCTIONS

Combine all ingredients in a food processor for 20 seconds, scrape down the flanks and mix for an extra quarter of a minute. Skipping a meal in the morning can make you feel starving at mid-morning and dream about tempting unhealthy food. So sip this up and dream about soy drink instead. This recipe is good for one person.

Each glass contains:

Calories – 350

Fat - 3.5 grams

Saturated fat - 0.1 gram

Sodium - 192 mg

Carbs - 74 grams

Sugars - 44 grams

Fiber - 7 grams

Protein - 9 grams

# Mango Folly

INGREDIENTS

- 1 can of 8 ounces juice-packed pineapple chunks
- 1 cup fat-free frozen vanilla yogurt
- 1 large peeled and chopped ripe mango
- 1 sliced ripe banana
- Crushed or cracked ice

INSTRUCTIONS

Combine the banana, pineapple with juice, mango and frozen yogurt and blend until even. Then gradually pop in the ice to make the mixture reach the level for four cups. Blend until the ice stays pureed and serve to two people. Do well from the disease fighting ability of ripe mangoes with this delightful drink.

Each glass contains:

Calories – 251

Fat - 0.5 grams

Saturated fat - 0.2 gram

Sodium - 68 mg

Carbs - 60 grams

Sugars - 50 grams

Fiber - 4 grams

Protein - 6.5 grams

## Super Green

INGREDIENTS

- 1¼ cups chopped kale leaves without tough rib and stems

- 1¼ cups frozen cubed mango

- 2 chopped medium ribs celery
- 1 cup cold fresh orange or tangerine juice
- ¼ cup chopped flat-leaf parsley
- ¼ cup chopped fresh mint

INSTRUCTIONS

Combine all in a blender, puree until even and pout into two chilled glasses. The parsley and celery that back up its cheerful green shade are diuretics, which help wash away toxins from your body. Mango and kale are superb foods bursting together with nutrition to support cleansing of the physique.

Each glass contains:

Calories – 160

Protein - 3 grams

Carbs - 39 grams

Fiber - 5 grams

Fat - 0.5 gram

Sodium - 56 mg

# Healthy Kale

INGREDIENTS

- 1 pear
- ¼ avocado
- 1 cucumber
- ½ of a lemon
- A handful of cilantro
- 1 cup packed kale
- ½ inch ginger
- 2 cups coconut water
- 1 scoop protein powder
- Pure water

INSTRUCTIONS

Blend all ingredients and serve to four people. These potent detox drinks keep inside the refrigerator for 24 hours only. A cup of kale has no fat, only 36 calories, and is high with antioxidants and vitamins.

## Sweet Soul

INGREDIENTS

- ½ of a banana
- ½ cup blueberries
- ¼ avocado
- ½ cup almond milk
- 1 tsp spirulina
- 1 scoop vanilla protein powder
- Pure water

INSTRUCTIONS

Blend all and serve to two people. Do not fear its dim colour, as well as its mossy odour as spirulina, a kind of micro-algae, is an extra-large healing detox representative.

## Smoothie Bliss

INGREDIENTS

- Pear
- Avocado
- 1 packed cup spinach
- 3/4 cup coconut water
- 1 cup almond milk
- 1 tsp chia seeds
- 1 scoop protein powder
- Pure water

INSTRUCTIONS

Blend all and serve to three people. A teaspoon of chia seeds stores almost two grams of dietary fiber and lots of omega-3.

## Smooth Green Drink

INGREDIENTS

- 5 large Romaine lettuce leaves
- ½ of a Granny Smith apple
- ¼ avocado
- ½ of a cucumber
- ½ cup jicama
- Handful of cilantro
- 1 whole lime
- 4 scoops of hemp protein

- 1 Medjool date
- Pure water

INSTRUCTIONS

Blend all and serve to two people. This green drink brings out the crispy root veggie jicama, which is rife with vitamin C. Jicama resembles an extremely large brown turnip or potato and high in fiber, which is significant to peptic health and contributes towards lowering cholesterol.

## Crazy Sensual Goddess

INGREDIENTS

- 1 avocado or coconut meat or raw almond butter or nut milk
- 1 banana
- 1 cup blueberries

- 1 cucumber
- A fistful of kale or romaine or spinach
- Coconut water or purified water
- Stevia, to taste
- A sprinkle of cinnamon or some cacao (optional)

INSTRUCTIONS

In high speed setting, blend altogether the ingredients till smooth and serve to two people. The coconut water, avocado, greens and cucumber will bathe your cells with alkalizing heavens. High pH inner environs help the systems of the body operate at its best.

## Strawberry Meadows

INGREDIENTS

- 3 cups of your preferred nondairy milk

- 2 cups garden-fresh strawberries
- 1 tablespoon zest of lemon
- 1 peeled small orange
- 1 banana
- 1½ cups loosely packed spinach

INSTRUCTIONS

In high speed setting, blend altogether the ingredients until smooth and serve to two people. Strawberries exists as phytonutrient plants, supplying your physique with an abundance of antioxidant and anti-inflammatory nutrients

## Sicilian Carrot

INGREDIENTS

- 6 carrots

- 3 large tomatoes
- 2 red bell peppers
- 4 cloves garlic
- 4 stalks celery
- 1 cup watercress
- 1 cup loosely packed spinach
- 1 red jalapeño, seeded (optional)

INSTRUCTIONS

Wash and prepare all ingredients for processing. This energetic, spicy smoothie fills you up once your stomach starts grumbling. Celery is a fabulous phthalate and phytochemical.

## Blue Lemon

INGREDIENTS

- 1 cup alkaline water
- ¼ cup organic blueberries
- 1 whole organic lemon

INSTRUCTIONS

Blend altogether the constituents inside a blender and serve to only one person. This simple to prepare recipe improvements immunity, aids relieve kidney stone discomfort, sore throat, scurvy, constipation, canker wounds and disorders in the gums.

## Strawberry Goji

INGREDIENTS

- 1 cup of coconut water
- 1 icy banana
- ¼ cup chilled strawberries

- 3 tablespoons Goji berries

INSTRUCTIONS

Blend the entire components together in a food processor. You'll enjoy this smoothie as it has superfood nutrition, and aphrodisiac properties as well!

## Blue Ginger

INGREDIENTS

- 1 cup milk of your choice
- ¼ cup blueberries
- 1 frozen banana
- 3 tablespoons ginger juice

INSTRUCTIONS

Blend all in a food processor and serve to one person. Blueberries are high in antioxidants and great in nutrition.

## Mint Berry

INGREDIENTS

- ½ of a green apple
- 2 tablespoons of Hemp Hearts
- 8 fresh mint leaves
- 4 leaves of organic green leaf lettuce
- ¼ cup unprocessed garden-fresh or refrigerated berry mixture
- 12 ounces pure water

INSTRUCTIONS

Blend all and serve to two people on top of ice cubes or crushed ice. Guzzle this in the morning and the protein would keep you feeling full until lunch. Mint exists as a good palate cleanser or appetizer and promotes worthy nutrition.

## Sexy Detox

INGREDIENTS

- 1 tablespoon of cacao powder
- 2 tablespoons of hemp seeds
- 5 red endive leaves
- Pinch of green stevia
- ¼ cup of unprocessed fresh or refrigerated dark red cherries
- 12 ounces pure water

INSTRUCTIONS

Blend all and serve to two people to sip themselves into becoming sexy. Endive is a salad veggie that has great vitamin A content that assists in improving sight.

## Super Fresh Green

INGREDIENTS

- 1 green apple
- 1 teaspoon of barley grass juice powder
- 1 lemon
- 1 peeled cucumber
- 4 leaves of red leaf lettuce
- ¼ cup of organic fresh or frozen mango
- 12 ounces pure water

INSTRUCTIONS

Blend all parts and serve to two people atop of cube or crushed ice. Barley grass, a grain heavy on nutrients, can aid and soothe pain and inflammation. It is among the list of plants with the highest organic levels of the enzyme, SOD or superoxide dismutase, which is a potent antioxidant.

## Glowing Blast

INGREDIENTS

- 25 pieces spinach
- ½ of a small cucumber
- 1 cored and deseeded pear
- 1 peeled lemon
- 1 peeled orange
- 1 tablespoon pumpkin seeds
- Water to the maximum line of the blender

INSTRUCTIONS

Blend all materials and serve to one person atop ice cubes or crushed ice. Pumpkin seeds contain magnesium, a crystal that may improve sleep, besides keeping migraines away.

## Clear Sip Smoothie

INGREDIENTS

- 1 cup coconut kefir
- ½ cup full stems and leaves of flat-leaf parsley
- 1 cucumber without seeds
- 1 apple
- 1 tablespoon coconut oil
- 1 lime
- 2 tablespoons garden-fresh mint leaves

## INSTRUCTIONS

Blend all and serve to one person atop ice cubes. This is a golden sticker to an unblemished complexion aside from being gluten-free. Coconut kefir reinstates radiance through living probiotics. Parsley, on the other hand, oxygenates, while cucumber refreshes, coconut oil conditions, lime delivers toning vitamin C, as well as mint stores vitamin A, which reinforces skin tissues and supports reducing oil in the skin.

## Berry Pick-Me-Up

### INGREDIENTS

- 1 cup coconut milk
- 1 cup blueberries
- ½ cup raspberries
- ½ cup blackberries

- 2 tablespoons Goji berries or 1 tablespoon of Goji powder

- 1 tablespoon coconut oil

- 1 tablespoon ground flax seed

- 2 pitted dates

INSTRUCTIONS

If using Goji berries, soak it in water for a quarter of an hour before processing. Blend all and serve to one person with ice cubes. We are all going gaga aimed at antioxidant-rich goji as studies had shown that it may reduce stress and fatigue.

## Forever Young

INGREDIENTS

- 1 cup coconut water

- 3 stalks of kale
- Handful of spinach
- ½ cup filled with leaves and stems of flat-leaf parsley
- ½ cup cilantro leaves and stems
- 2 green apples
- ¼ tsp fresh grated ginger
- 2 heaping tablespoons of wild blue-green algae

INSTRUCTIONS

Blend all and serve to one person. This is another great alkalized smoothie with blue-green algae chocking it full of protein to provide the essential amino acids.

## Cranberry Smoothie

INGREDIENTS

- ½ cup cranberries
- 1 large celery stalk
- 1 cucumber
- 1 apple
- 1 pear
- Handful of spinach

INSTRUCTIONS

Process all and serve to one person over ice cubes to sip this chilly detox smoothie and have strong kidneys.

## Fat Booty Buster

INGREDIENTS

- 1 medium organic red beet
- 3 medium organic carrots

- 1 organic radish
- 2 organic garlic cloves
- Large handful of organic parsley

INSTRUCTIONS

Process all ingredients in a food processor and serve to one person over ice cubes. If a firm flat belly exists on top of your list of wishes, start through this extreme cleansing smoothie.

## Berry Pomegranate Smoothie

INGREDIENTS

- 2 cups frozen mixed berries
- 1 cup pomegranate juice
- 1 medium banana
- 1/2 cup nonfat cottage cheese

- 1/2 cup water

INSTRUCTIONS

Combine all ingredients in a food processor and blend until smooth. Serve to two people immediately.

Each glass contains:

Calories – 206

Fat - 1 gram

Cholesterol - 3 mg

Carbs - 49 grams

Protein - 6 grams

Fiber - 6 grams

Sodium - 133 mg

Potassium - 625 mg

# Gentle Wind

INGREDIENTS

- 1 chopped small cucumber
- 2 peeled ripe kiwis
- 1 cup ginger-flavored Kombucha
- 1/2 cup low-fat plain Greek yogurt
- 2 tablespoons fresh cilantro leaves
- 6 ice cubes

INSTRUCTIONS

Combine all ingredients in a blender and process until even. Serve to two people immediately.

Each glass contains:

Calories – 116

Fat - 2 grams

Cholesterol - 4 mg

Carbs - 21 grams

Added sugars - 1 gram

Protein - 6 grams

Fiber - 3 grams

Sodium - 32 mg

Potassium - 424 mg

# Hawaiian Drink

INGREDIENTS

- 1 cup chopped fresh pineapple
- 1/2 cup chopped peeled papaya
- 1/4 cup guava nectar
- 1 tablespoon lime juice
- 1 teaspoon grenadine

- 1/2 cup ice

INSTRUCTIONS

Place the ingredients within the sequence listed inside a food processor. Pulse three times towards chopping the fruits, then process until even. Serve to two people immediately. For the finest color and taste, use a red-meat Hawaiian papaya aimed at this unusual, lip-puckering flavor of islet summer.

Papayas are loaded with papain, a gastric enzyme, making this drink a great dessert towards settling stomachs following a heavy meal.

Each glass contains:

Calories – 81

Carbs - 21 grams

Protein - 1 gram

Fiber - 2 grams

Sodium - 5 mg

Potassium - 201 mg

# Part 2

# Introduction

Are you tired of complicated diet programs that don't give you results? Do you want a quick and easy way to loose weight, have more energy and be healthier? Do you want some tips to begin a journey in the smoothie world? If this is what your looking for, then you're in the right place!

This book contains proven steps and strategies on how to make the best smoothies – those that make you much healthier in as short as 14 days!

Smoothies are among the best "tools" to get the daily recommended intake of fruits and vegetables. They provide almost all of the essential nutrients needed for better health. They improve digestion, cleanse the body, boost the immune system, and promote overall wellbeing.

They are also the best aid to weight loss. Smoothies are low in calories and they can replace a meal or two. With smoothies, losing weight without sacrificing complete and balanced nutrition is not just possible – it's actually easy.

By the way, this book contains a list of the best smoothie ingredients for weight loss. Although most smoothie ingredients are healthy, not all are ideal for your pound-shedding pursuits. If you don't pay much attention to the combination of ingredients, you may actually come up with a recipe for weight gain.

This book also features some of the best smoothie recipes that are easy to prepare, making them perfect for beginners. You'll also find various smoothie-making tips, which will keep you away from the hassles of learning. In other words, you're guaranteed to have fun as you begin your Smoothie Adventure!

Thanks again for downloading this book, I hope you enjoy it!

# Chapter 1: Smoothies With Benefits

Who doesn't love delicious, thirst-quenching smoothies? There's no denying that smoothies have become popular. They have won the hearts of many because they are not just tasty – they're nutritious too. Because of their various benefits, they have also made their way to the kitchens of many health-conscious individuals.

**Promote Weight Loss**

It's not a secret. The only reason why smoothies can make a person lose weight is because they make a person feel fuller without consuming added calories. A glass of smoothie typically contains only around 200 to 300 calories. So if a meal will be substituted with a smoothie, there will about 20% to 30% reduction in the total daily calorie intake. When the body has a high caloric deficit, it will start to burn stored body fat.

It must be understood that unused calories will be stored as fat in the body. Having lower calorie intake translates to having less fat to burn or store. This will result in effective weight loss in just a few weeks.

In addition, it is also easy to control the calorie content of smoothies. For one, most smoothie ingredients are naturally low in calories. Second, the ingredients can be mixed in order to make more filling blends without the extra calories. Lastly, a variety of add-ons can boost their fat-burning properties.

Detoxify the Body

Detoxification is important for the body to stay in good shape. Every day, the body is exposed to pollutants and other harmful chemicals. The toxins can come from the air, food, water, and even household and beauty products. If these toxins pile up in the body, they could cause serious health issues in the long run.

Our body has its own ways of flushing out toxins, but we can help it eliminate toxic substances faster – ant that's by drinking smoothies. Smoothies are packed with phytochemicals that effectively bind with toxins and flush them out.

The body will be cleansed a little bit each day by drinking detoxifying smoothies. Detoxification is not a one-day process. So, be patient and you'll soon see that a detox day will go a long way.

Provide Energy for the Body

Most often, people who feel sluggish turn to sugar-loaded food and caffeinated drinks to get a much-needed energy boost. But sugary foods can only provide a temporary surge of energy. The best way to combat low energy is to follow a balanced diet.

However, with their fast-paced lifestyle, people don't get the nutrients they need for the day ahead. With smoothies, they can get all the essential nutrients in just one glass.

Smoothies contain the right combination of carbohydrate, protein, and healthy fats that the body needs for energy. They also contain most of the vitamins and minerals needed for proper body processes.

Smoothies can be blended with additional adaptogens or stress-busting herbs. The herbs can effectively restore balance in the adrenal glands and promote homeostasis in the body.

Boost the Immune System

The body's immune system is the first barrier against infection. It keeps disease-causing bacteria and viruses from invading the body. So, it is imperative to keep the immune system healthy all the time.

The immune system needs lots of vitamins A, B, C, D and E to function well. It also needs minerals such as zinc and selenium. By having the right ingredients, smoothies can boost immunity.

# Chapter 2: How To Make Smoothies?

Now that you know what smoothies can do, it's time to learn the basics of smoothie-making. Making healthy smoothies is really easy. All it takes is a little creativity in mixing, matching, and blending of the right ingredients. It can even be likened to art.

It doesn't have to be complicated. Here are the simple steps to make the perfect smoothie:

Choose a Smoothie Base

Creaminess is one of the best characteristics of a good smoothie. To give the smoothie creamy goodness, you'll to choose the perfect base.

Fruits are ideal for smoothies because they provide the right creaminess. They also add a natural sweetness to the blend. Banana and apple are the most popular fruits for smoothies. Other terrific fruits that will make smoothies creamy are coconut meat, mango, and avocado.

You don't want your smoothies to be runny. So avoid using fruits with high water content like pineapple, watermelon, and cantaloupe. If there is really a need to use them, add ice to adjust the consistency of the blend.

Choose the Liquid

The next thing to do is to choose the liquid to be added. The right kind of liquid will not only affect the overall taste of the blend, it will also affect the consistency. Usually, smoothies need about one to two cups of liquid, depending on the ingredients used.

The best liquids to use are coconut water, coconut milk, almond milk, tea, and plain water. Yogurt, kefir, and ice are also perfect for use in adjusting the consistency of the smoothies.

Choose the Main Ingredients

Use fresh fruits. Frozen fruits are okay too. If the recipe calls for vegetables, it is best to use the fresh ones. People who are not used to eating vegetables may opt to start with fruity smoothies. Later on, they could try to experiment and make a

smoothie that's a combination of fruit and vegetable. Eventually, their taste buds will get used to all-vegetable smoothies.

Choose Any Add-ons

Some add-ons like sweeteners, salt, and spices can make the smoothies tastier. Protein powders and superfoods, on the other hand, can make the smoothies much more nutritious.

Almost all smoothie recipes are compatible with these add-ons. So, have fun and improve your own smoothies as you please.

Choose a Blender

If you don't have the luxury of time, choose a high-speed blender. There are blenders which come with a smoothie button for easy and handy smoothie-making. However, any blender would do. There is no need to make a big fuss about it.

Smoothies with hard ingredients may need to be blended at low speed first. Most smoothies take about one to two minutes to blend. Depending on the amount of the ingredients, the smoothies may need to be blended for an extra minute in order to achieve the best results.

# Chapter 3: Smoothie Ingredients For Weight Loss

Not all nutritious ingredients support weight loss. Some ingredients are just better than others when it comes to speeding up the body's ability to burn fat. Here are the best smoothie ingredients for weight loss:

Fruits

- Avocado is one of the preferred fruits for weight loss; it curbs hunger, after all. It contains a good combination of unsaturated fats that make the stomach feel fuller for longer.
- Banana is another great smoothie thickener. It contains only about 100 calories but it fills up the stomach. It also contains naturally-occurring sugar that provides natural sweetness to smoothies.
- Apple is also a good smoothie base. A medium apple contains about 120 calories and about 6 grams of fiber. Fiber can keep the stomach satiated until the next meal, protecting you from the urge to snack on calorie-rich food.
- Berries provide tons of flavor to smoothies, without the unwanted calories. All kinds of berries such as blueberry, raspberry, strawberry, and blackberry are all-time smoothie favorites. They have high fiber content and they have plenty of antioxidants too.

Leafy Greens

- Spinach goes well with smoothies. A cup of spinach contains only seven calories but it is packed with essential vitamins and minerals for good health.
- Kale is another smoothie powerhouse ingredient. A cup of kale contains about thirty calories. It is high in isothiocyanates, a phytonutrient which has a detoxifying power that aids in weight loss.
- Chard has a mild flavor so it's perfect for smoothies. A cup of this vegetable contains twenty calories and four grams of fiber. So, it's great for weight loss too.

Liquids

o Tea is high in catechins, a substance that promotes faster fat metabolism. A cup of tea contains only one calorie.
o Coconut water is refreshing. It is loaded with bioactive enzymes that promote better and faster metabolism of lipids. A cup of coconut water contains about six calories.
o Almond milk is the best substitute for dairy milk. It contains no fat and one cup of it contains only thirty calories. Its gives smoothies a unique nutty flavor as well as a tempting aroma.
o Coconut milk is another great milk substitute. A cup of it contains about 200 calories and a high amount of healthy fats.
o Greek yogurt is the best substitute for high-fat creams. It is high in protein which fills up the stomach, making it feel full for longer. It also

contains probiotics that aid in digestion. A cup of plain Greek yogurt has about 60 calories.

Add-ons

- o Coconut oil contains healthy fats that aid the body in losing weight. Most of the fats in coconut oil are MCTs or medium-chain triglycerides. The fats are instantly used by the body as energy. So, it means they don't get to be stored as body fat. They also curb hunger and lessen the need to consume more calories.
- o Nut butters are also great add-ons. They don't just add nutty flavors to smoothies; they also make the consistency more creamy and smooth. They also have healthy fats that help the body lose some more weight. Nut butters that go well with smoothies are hazelnut butter, almond butter, peanut butter, and cashew butter.
- o Chia seeds are perfect for weight loss. Their high protein content keeps the stomach feel full for longer. Aside from being packed with nutrients, they are also rich in antioxidants.

- Cinnamon is a spice that promotes rapid weight loss. It effectively regulates blood sugar metabolism, preventing sugar from being stored as fat.
- Cayenne pepper is another spice that can help shed off some pounds. This spice contains high amounts of capsaicin, which effectively curbs hunger. Adding

cayenne pepper to morning smoothies reduces the need to consume more calories later in the day.
- Sweeteners can be added to smoothies to enhance the taste. Opt for natural sweeteners. Stevia is the best natural sweetener because it contains zero calories. Other natural sweeteners such as honey, dates, and maple syrup contain calories, so they should be used in moderation.

Ingredients to Avoid

- Dairy – Milk, cream, and other dairy products can really make great-tasting smoothies. However, they are also loaded with calories. If losing weight is a goal, then staying away from them is a must.
- Canned fruits and vegetables – Fresh and organic fruits and vegetables are highly recommended for making the best smoothies. If they are not available, better choose the frozen ones over those that are canned. Always keep in mind that canned food contain additional sodium and sugar, which are not beneficial for weight loss.
- Fruit juice – Store-bought fruit juice contains added sugar. Even freshly- squeezed fruit juice can contain lots of natural sugar. Simply put, the more sugar a smoothie has, the more calorie-loaded it is.
- Sweet fruits –There is no question about fruits being good for health. Still, if too much of them will be used for smoothies, they will lead to weight gain instead. Sweet fruits have high sugar content which can increase blood sugar levels, leading to more

sugar being stored as fat. Sweet fruits like apple, banana, and mango must be used in moderation. Other fruits high in sugar are pineapple, grape, fig, and pomegranate.

# Chapter 4: Beginners Plan. Smoothie Recipes For Days 1 To 7

It's time to get started. But before you embark on the 14-day smoothie adventure, you must understand that there are some nasty things you may encounter.

Drinking smoothies could make you undergo heavy detox during the first few days. So, frequent urination and diarrhea may be experienced. Your body's caloric deficit can also cause induction flu. Symptoms of induction flu include headache, nausea, and upset stomach. However, these symptoms are just temporary and may go away after a few days.

So for the first week, don't rush things. Start slowly and drink just the right amount of smoothies. Start with two to three glasses of smoothies daily. Ideally, two glasses of smoothie should be taken in the morning. They should replace the regular breakfast meal. Another glass of smoothie can be taken as a snack in the afternoon.

Here are some easy-to-make fruity smoothies. Choose one recipe for breakfast and one for the afternoon snack.

# Day One

## Spiced Apple Smoothie

Ingredients:

- 1 apple
- 1 banana
- 1 tablespoon honey
- ¼ cup plain yogurt
- ½ cup almond milk
- 1 teaspoon cinnamon
- ½ teaspoon ginger, grated
- ¼ teaspoon nutmeg
- ½ cup ice

Procedure:

Remove the seeds of the apple. Chop banana and apple into small pieces. Place the ice, apple, banana, almond milk, yogurt, ginger, cinnamon, and nutmeg into the blender. Pulse for 30 seconds. Add honey and pulse for another 10 seconds, or until smooth. Transfer the smoothie into a glass. Sprinkle cinnamon on top and then serve immediately.

# Three Berry Smoothie

Ingredients:

- ½ cup raspberries
- ½ cup blueberries
- ½ cup blackberries
- ½ cup rolled oats
- ½ cup plain yogurt
- ½ cup almond milk
- 1 tablespoon honey or stevia
- ½ cup ice

Procedure:

Put all the berries, almond milk, yogurt, rolled oats, and ice in the blender. Blend at high speed for five seconds. Add honey and continue to blend until ice has been crushed. Add a little water if it's too thick. Pulse for another five seconds, or until mixture is smooth. Transfer into a glass and serve immediately.

# Day Two

## Spiced Banana Smoothie

Ingredients:

- 1 frozen banana
- ½ cup almond milk
- 1 teaspoon cinnamon
- ¼ teaspoon nutmeg
- 1 tablespoon honey or stevia
- 1 teaspoon vanilla extract
- 1 tablespoon shaved chocolate
- ½ cup ice

Procedure:

Place banana, almond milk, cinnamon, nutmeg, vanilla extract, and ice in the blender. Blend at high speed for one minute. Add honey and continue to blend for 5 seconds. Add shaved chocolate and blend for another five seconds. Transfer smoothie into a mason jar. Garnish with shaved chocolate and some banana slices. Serve.

# Very Cherry Smoothie

Ingredients:

- 1 cup frozen cherries
- ½ cup almond milk
- ½ cup plain yogurt
- 1 tablespoon honey
- ¼ teaspoon almond extract


- ¼ teaspoon vanilla extract
- ¼ cup rolled oats
- ¼ cup ice

Procedure:

Add cherries, almond milk, yogurt, almond extract, vanilla extract, honey, and rolled oats to a blender. Pulse for thirty seconds. Adjust consistency by adding ice. Add a pinch of salt. Continue to pulse for another thirty seconds. Pour smoothie into a glass and then serve immediately.

# Day Three

Coco Brownie Smoothie

Ingredients:

- 1 banana
- ¼ cup unsweetened coconut flakes
- ¼ cup graham cracker, crushed
- ½ cup coconut milk
- 1 tablespoon honey or stevia
- 1 tablespoon coconut oil
- ½ cup ice

Procedure:

Add banana, graham cracker, coconut milk, and ice to a blender. Pulse it for thirty seconds or until smooth. Add coconut flakes and honey, then pulse for ten seconds. Add coconut oil and then pulse for another ten seconds. Transfer the smoothie into a tall glass. Top with coconut flakes and crushed graham. Serve and enjoy.

# Berry Red Smoothie

Ingredients:

- 1 cup strawberries
- 1 banana
- 1 small beet
- ½ cup coconut water
- 1 tablespoon coconut oil
- ½ cup ice
- 1 tablespoon honey

Procedure:

Chop the strawberries and banana. Scrub, trim, and then chop the beet. Place strawberries, beet, banana, coconut water, and ice in the blender. Blend at high speed for thirty seconds. Add coconut oil and honey. Add two to three strawberries for added texture and then continue to blend for ten seconds. Serve immediately.

# Day Four

## Easy Blueberry Smoothie

Ingredients:

- 1 cup blueberries
- ½ cup almond milk
- ½ cup plain yogurt
- 1 banana, chopped
- 1 tablespoon honey or stevia
- 2 tablespoons almonds, chopped
- 2 tablespoons unsweetened coconut flakes

Procedure:

Add banana, blueberries, almond milk, yogurt, almonds, and coconut flakes to the blender. Blend at high speed for one minute, or until smooth. Add honey and continue to blend for another ten seconds. Transfer smoothie into a tall glass and top with coconut flakes. Serve and enjoy.

# Choco Peanut Smoothie

Ingredients:

- 3 tablespoons peanut butter
- 1 frozen banana
- 1 tablespoon cocoa powder
- 1 tablespoon honey
- ½ cup almond milk
- ½ cup ice

Procedure:

Place banana, peanut butter, cocoa powder, almond milk, and ice to the blender. Blend at high speed for 30 seconds. Add honey to the mixture and continue to blend until smooth. Add more ice to adjust consistency. Transfer smoothie into a mason jar. Sprinkle cocoa powder on top and then serve.

# Day Five

## Avocado Mango Smoothie

Ingredients:

- 1 avocado, pitted and chopped
- 1 mango, pitted and chopped
- 1 cup green tea (brewed and cooled)
- 1 cup spinach
- 1 tablespoon honey
- 1 tablespoon coconut oil
- ¼ teaspoon salt
- ½ cup ice

Procedure:

Add avocado, mango, spinach, green tea, and ice to the blender. Puree for one minute until mixture is smooth. Add honey and salt and then continue to puree for thirty seconds. Add coconut oil and pulse for five seconds. Serve immediately.

# Nutty Raspberry Smoothie

Ingredients:

- 1 cup raspberries
- 1 banana, chopped
- ½ cup coconut milk
- ¼ cup unsweetened coconut flakes
- 1 tablespoon coconut oil
- 1 tablespoon chia seeds
- ½ cup ice

Procedure:

Add raspberries, banana, coconut milk, coconut flakes, and ice to the blender. Blend for one minute. Add chia seeds and continue to blend for ten seconds. Add the coconut oil and blend for five seconds more. Transfer smoothie into a jar or glass. Garnish with coconut flakes and then serve.

# Day Six

## Berry Avocado Smoothie

Ingredients:

- 1 avocado, pitted and chopped
- ½ cup blueberries
- 1 tablespoon coconut oil
- 1 tablespoon chia seeds
- ½ tablespoon honey or stevia
- ½ teaspoon cinnamon
- ½ cup ice

Procedure:

Place avocado, blueberries, cinnamon, and ice in a blender. Blend at high speed for thirty seconds. Add honey and chia seeds and then continue to blend for thirty seconds. Add coconut oil and blend for ten seconds more. Pour smoothie in a glass and then sprinkle cinnamon on top. Serve immediately.

# Savory Carrot Smoothie

Ingredients:

- 1 carrot
- 1 medium-sized banana
- ½ cup plain yogurt
- ½ cup almond milk
- ½ teaspoon cinnamon
- ½ teaspoon nutmeg
- 1 tablespoon honey or stevia
- 1 tablespoon cashew nuts, chopped

Procedure:

Peel carrot and banana. Chop them into small pieces. Place carrot, banana, almond milk, yogurt, cinnamon, nutmeg, and ice in a blender. Blend at high speed for thirty to sixty seconds. Add honey and cashew nuts to the mixture and then blend for another ten seconds. Transfer the smoothie into a glass. Garnish with grated carrots and chopped cashew nuts. Serve immediately.

## Day Seven

## Berry Chia Smoothie

Ingredients:

- 1 cup strawberries
- ½ cup pomegranate juice, unsweetened
- 1 tablespoon chia seeds
- ½ cup ice

Procedure:

Place strawberries, juice, chia seeds, and ice in a blender. Blend at high speed for about thirty seconds. Add chia seeds and blend for another thirty seconds. Serve immediately.

# Berry Nutty Smoothie

Ingredients:

- ½ cup strawberries
- ½ cup blueberries
- ½ cup plain yogurt
- ¼ cup almonds
- ½ cup ice

Procedure:

Add strawberries, blueberries, banana, yogurt, and ice to the blender. Blend at high speed for about thirty seconds. Add the almonds and blend for another thirty seconds. Pour smoothie in a glass. Top with chopped almonds then serve.

# Chapter 5: Smoothie Recipes For Days 8 To 14

During the second week, your body is likely to have adjusted already to the smoothie diet. The flu-like symptoms are expected to be gone. Your weight is also expected to drop anywhere between two to ten pounds.

The second week is the best time to experiment more on what extras to include in the smoothies. Your smoothie intake can be gradually increased to four glasses or one liter. The smoothies can replace a meal or two, preferably breakfast and dinner.

Below are some smoothies that contain mixed fruits and vegetable. Choose one recipe for breakfast and one for dinner.

# Day Eight

## Coco Raspberry Smoothie

Ingredients:

- 2 teaspoons coconut oil
- ½ cup coconut milk
- ¼ cup unsweetened coconut flakes
- ½ cup raspberries
- 1 medium-sized banana
- ½ cup cucumber, chopped
- ¼ cup ice

Procedure:

Slice the banana into small pieces. Add the banana and the coconut milk to the blender and then blend at high speed for five seconds. Add the ice, raspberries, and coconut flakes to the mixture and continue to blend for 30 seconds, or until smooth. Add the coconut oil and then pulse for another 10 seconds. Transfer smoothie into a mason jar. Garnish with coconut flakes and then serve.

# Creamy Blueberry Smoothie

Ingredients:

- 1 cup frozen blueberries
- 1 frozen banana
- ½ cup chard, chopped
- ¼ cup almond butter
- ½ cup almond milk
- ½ cup plain yogurt
- ½ cup ice

Procedure:

Add banana, blueberries, almond milk, almond butter, yogurt, and ice to the blender. Blend at high speed for one minute or until smooth. Add a little water to adjust the consistency. Serve and enjoy.

# Day Nine

## Coco Choco Smoothie

Ingredients:

- ½ cup coconut milk
- ½ cup almond milk
- 2 tablespoons cacao powder
- 2 tablespoons unsweetened coconut flakes
- 1 medium-sized banana
- ½ cup cucumber, chopped
- 2 dates pitted
- ½ cup ice

Procedure:

Place banana, dates, almond milk, coconut milk, and cacao powder in a blender. Puree for 30 seconds or until smooth. Add coconut flakes and continue to puree for another five seconds. Pour smoothie in a mason jar or glass. Top with coconut flakes and cacao powder. Serve and enjoy.

# Apple Kale Smoothie

Ingredients:

- 1 cup kale, chopped
- 1 frozen banana
- ½ cup apple cider
- ½ teaspoon cinnamon
- 1 tablespoon pecans, chopped
- 2 teaspoons almond butter
- ½ cup ice

Procedure:

Add kale, banana, apple cider, cinnamon, almond butter, and ice to the blender. Puree for about one minute. Add pecans. Add more ice if needed. Continue to puree for another 10 seconds. Pour smoothie in a jar. Sprinkle cinnamon and chopped pecans then serve.

# Day Ten

# All-Green Smoothie

Ingredients:

- 1 cup kale, chopped
- 1 avocado, pitted and chopped
- 1 apple, cored and chopped
- ½ cup broccoli florets, chopped
- ½ cup zucchini, chopped
- ¼ cup parsley, chopped
- 1 tablespoon fresh lime juice
- 2 teaspoons chia seeds
- ½ cup almond milk
- ½ cup ice

Procedure:

Place all ingredients, except the chia seeds, in a blender. Blend at high speed for one minute or until smooth. Add chia seeds and give it a quick stir before serving.

# Mint Green Smoothie

Ingredients:

- 1 banana, chopped
- ½ cup cucumber, chopped
- 2 tablespoons fennel bulb, chopped
- ¼ teaspoon spirulina
- 1 teaspoon ginger, grated
- 1 sprig mint
- ½ cup coconut water


- 1 tablespoon honey or stevia
- ½ cup ice

Procedure:

Add banana, cucumber, fennel bulb, ginger, coconut water, mint, and ice to a blender. Blend all ingredients for one minute, or until smooth. Add spirulina and honey then continue to blend for thirty seconds. Pour smoothie in a tall glass. Garnish with mint leaves and then serve.

# Day Eleven

## Spiced Green Apple Smoothie

Ingredients:

- 1 green apple
- 1 cup baby spinach
- ½ teaspoon cinnamon
- ¼ teaspoon cardamom
- ½ teaspoon vanilla extract
- 1 tablespoon honey or stevia

Procedure:

Cut the apples into small pieces. Place the apple, spinach, cinnamon, cardamom, vanilla extract, and ice in a blender. Pulse for one minute, or until mixture is smooth. Add honey and continue to blend for ten seconds. Pour smoothie in a glass and sprinkle cinnamon on top before serving.

# Tangy Minty Green Smoothie

Ingredients:

- ½ cup baby spinach
- 1 stalk kale
- ¼ cup parsley
- 1 sprig mint
- ½ of cucumber
- ½ of apple or pear
- 2 tablespoons fresh lemon juice
- 1 teaspoon ginger, grated
- ¼ cup ice

Procedure:

Trim kale and chop it roughly. Peel the cucumber and chop it. Add kale, spinach, cucumber, mint, parsley, ginger, and ice to the blender. Blend ingredients for one minute or until ice is broken up. Add lemon juice and continue to blend for 30 seconds, or until everything is well incorporated. Pour smoothie into a mason jar and garnish with chopped mint. Serve immediately.

# Day Twelve

## Coco Kale Smoothie

Ingredients:

- 1 cup kale, chopped
- 2 tablespoons unsweetened coconut flakes
- 1 cup coconut water
- 1 cup blueberries
- 2 tablespoons chia seeds
- ½ cup ice

Procedure:

Add kale, blueberries, coconut water, blueberries, chia seeds, and ice to a blender. Blend at high speed for one minute. Add coconut flakes and blend for five seconds. Pour smoothie in a tall glass. Top with coconut flakes then serve immediately.

# Sweet Green Tea Smoothie

Ingredients:

- 1 tablespoon green tea powder or matcha
- 1 banana, chopped
- 1 avocado, pitted and chopped
- 1 cup spinach
- 1 sprig mint
- ½ cup almond milk
- 1 tablespoon shaved chocolate
- ½ cup ice

Procedure:

Add green tea, banana, avocado, spinach, mint, almond milk, and ice to a blender. Blend at high speed for thirty seconds. Add chia seeds and shaved chocolate then blend for five seconds. Transfer smoothie into a glass. Stir in some chia seeds. Top with shaved chocolate and then serve.

# Day Thirteen

# Spinach Berry Smoothie

Ingredients:

- ½ cup blueberries
- ½ cup blackberries
- 1 banana
- 1 cup baby spinach
- ¼ teaspoon cayenne pepper
- 1 tablespoon coconut oil
- ½ cup almond milk
- ½ cup ice

Procedure:

Place berries, banana, spinach, almond milk, and ice in a blender. Blend at high speed for thirty seconds. Add cayenne pepper and blend for another thirty seconds. Add coconut oil and blend for ten seconds. Pour smoothie into a mason jar then top with a pinch of cayenne pepper. Serve and enjoy.

# Creamy Blackberry Smoothie

Ingredients:

- 1 cup blackberries
- 1 banana, chopped
- 2 dates, pitted
- 1 apple, cored and chopped
- ½ cup plain yogurt
- ½ cup almond milk
- ½ teaspoon vanilla extract
- 1 teaspoon cinnamon
- 1 tablespoon ground flaxseed

Procedure:

Place blackberries, banana, apple, almond milk, yogurt, dates, flaxseed, and ice in a blender. Blend at high speed for one minute. Adjust consistency by adding ice. Add cinnamon and blend for ten seconds. Pour smoothie into a glass. Sprinkle cinnamon then serve immediately.

# Conclusion

Thank you again for downloading this book!

I hope this book was able to help you find the basic information to jumpstart your 14-day smoothie Adventure. I hope that you were able to get new ideas on how to make great-tasting and nutritious smoothies.

The next step is for you to apply what you've learned immediately, so that you can start to lose weight, feel great, and get energized as soon as possible.

Thank you and Good Luck!

www.ingramcontent.com/pod-product-compliance
Lightning Source LLC
Chambersburg PA
CBHW071438070526
44578CB00001B/134